KnockoutJS Essentials

Implement a successful JavaScript-rich application with KnockoutJS, jQuery, and Bootstrap

Jorge Ferrando

PUBLISHING

BIRMINGHAM - MUMBAI

KnockoutJS Essentials

First published: February 2015

Production reference: 1210215

Published by Packt Publishing Ltd.
Livery Place
35 Livery Street
Birmingham B3 2PB, UK.
ISBN 978-1-78439-707-4

www.packtpub.com

Credits

Author
Jorge Ferrando

Reviewers
Bhoomi Desai
Christian Droulers
Magesh Kuppan

Commissioning Editor
Dipika Gaonkar

Acquisition Editor
Owen Roberts

Content Development Editor
Shubhangi Dhamgaye

Technical Editor
Ruchi Desai

Copy Editors
Puja Lalwani
Laxmi Subramanian

Project Coordinator
Harshal Ved

Proofreaders
Simran Bhogal
Safis Editing
Paul Hindle

Indexer
Monica Ajmera Mehta

Graphics
Disha Haria

Production Coordinator
Nilesh R. Mohite

Cover Work
Nilesh R. Mohite

About the Author

Jorge Ferrando is a frontend developer at Uni Micro AS, Norway. He develops economy systems using JavaScript. He has experience as a PHP and C# developer working for companies such as Vigilant and Dreamstar Cash.

Jorge grew up in Callosa d'en Sarrià, Spain. He attended the University of Alicante where he discovered that web applications are his passion. He started to develop websites when he was 16 years old for a little company in his hometown. He then started practicing at Vigilant as a junior PHP developer; there, he created his first full web application and discovered the potential of JavaScript. Hard work lead him to a bigger company, Dreamstar Cash, also as a PHP developer. There, he got to know several good developers and began to work more and more with JavaScript; thanks to the company, who wanted to use Node.js, Jorge fell in love with JavaScript and frontend development. A few months later, he moved to Norway with his girlfriend and began to work with a company that gave him new challenges every day, working with KnockoutJS, AngularJS, and Twitter Bootstrap.

Acknowledgments

I can't believe how fortunate I was to work on this book with so many great people. I would like to say thank you to Ellen Bishop, who gave me the opportunity to write it, and Owen Roberts and Shubhangi Dhamgaye, who have led me in my first adventure as a writer. Also to Christian Droulers, I have learned very much with his reviews.

Firstly, I would like to say thank you to my family; they have always supported my dreams and have given me the freedom to fail and succeed by myself, and they have always been by my side taking care of me.

To my girlfriend, Teresa, who supported me in those hard days when I thought all is going to fall because I had work all around and just 24 hours in a day. She is my stone and my stability.

I would like to extend my gratitude to all the people I have learned something from: Manuel Ciges, who gave me the responsibility of making a full production application, and Marcos Fernández, my partner through that trip at Vigilant. Rafael Crisanto from Rc Informática, who gave me my first opportunity as a web developer. Pedro García, Pablo Deeleman, Javier Gómez, Fran Iruela, and Alfonso Fernández, my partners at Dreamstar Cash. Guys you made that time the best of my life and you have made me a better developer.

About the Reviewers

Bhoomi Desai is a technical enthusiast and is always keen to learn new technologies. She specializes in providing solutions for the cloud and web stacks. She is a software engineer by qualification and is yearning to become a software craftsman.

Bhoomi has strong technical expertise in coding standards, design patterns, refactoring, and UI design. She is a specialist in the JavaScript stack, Windows Azure, Amazon AWS, Node.js, and architectural patterns. Bhoomi is an early-curve technology adopter and an enthusiast for Agile and Lean development practices.

> I would like to thank my husband for always encouraging me to try new things in life.

Christian Droulers is a young and dynamic software developer who started programming in college and has not stopped since. Always on the lookout for interesting techniques and new patterns to apply in his everyday work, he's passionate about beautiful, clean, and efficient code.

He started his career developing key software applications for SherWeb, a renowned Microsoft hosting partner. Christian's passion and ability to decompose systems effectively led him to a software architect role, where he oversaw the complete rewrite of SherWeb's main application with asynchronous messaging, distributed systems, and recent frontend technologies.

Christian enjoys new challenges. In 2012, he joined up with three friends and cofounded Invup, a start-up aiming to help organizations track and quantify philanthropy. The start-up participated in the MassChallenge competition and came in as a finalist for the quality and innovative nature of their start-up. The company has now closed and the code is open sourced on Bitbucket.

He's currently working for the software consulting firm Vooban, heading a team of six developers working on a new platform for insurance management. He's also the author of a few public projects that are freely available at `http://cdroulers.com/projects/`. For Christian, software developing is not just a job; it's also a hobby and a way of life.

Magesh Kuppan is a freelance consultant and trainer on web technologies with over 17 years of experience. Everything about technology excites him.

> I am grateful to my parents, without whom I would not be what I am today. I am also thankful to my wife for she has been instrumental in all my efforts. Thanks to my little son who brings bliss to my life.

www.PacktPub.com

Support files, eBooks, discount offers, and more

For support files and downloads related to your book, please visit www.PacktPub.com.

Did you know that Packt offers eBook versions of every book published, with PDF and ePub files available? You can upgrade to the eBook version at www.PacktPub.com and as a print book customer, you are entitled to a discount on the eBook copy. Get in touch with us at service@packtpub.com for more details.

At www.PacktPub.com, you can also read a collection of free technical articles, sign up for a range of free newsletters and receive exclusive discounts and offers on Packt books and eBooks.

https://www2.packtpub.com/books/subscription/packtlib

Do you need instant solutions to your IT questions? PacktLib is Packt's online digital book library. Here, you can search, access, and read Packt's entire library of books.

Why subscribe?

- Fully searchable across every book published by Packt
- Copy and paste, print, and bookmark content
- On demand and accessible via a web browser

Free access for Packt account holders

If you have an account with Packt at www.PacktPub.com, you can use this to access PacktLib today and view 9 entirely free books. Simply use your login credentials for immediate access.

Table of Contents

Preface

One of the hardest problems to solve when we build the user interface is to synchronize data that developers manage behind the scenes, in the code, and data that is shown to the user. The first step that developers made was to separate the presentation and the logic. That separation allowed developers to manage both sides better and separately. But communication between these two layers still became hard. That was because JavaScript was considered a non-important language and we used to use it just for validation. Then jQuery gave us a clue about how powerful this language could be. But still data was managed in the server and we just displayed static presentations. That makes the user experience poor and slow.

Over the last few years, a new kind of architectural pattern has emerged. It is called the MVVM pattern. Libraries and frameworks that use this kind of pattern make it easy for developers to synchronize views and data. One of these libraries is Knockout, and the framework that uses Knockout is named Durandal.

Knockout is a fast and cross-browser-compatible library that helps us to develop client-side applications with a better user experience.

Developers don't need to worry any more about data synchronization. Knockout binds our code to the HTML elements showing the state of our code to the user in real time.

This dynamic binding makes us forget about coding synchronization, and we can focus our effort on coding the important features of our application.

Nowadays, managing these kinds of frameworks is a must for front-end developers. In this book, you will learn the basics of Knockout and Durandal and we will go into the best design practices and patterns of JavaScript.

If you want to improve the user experience of your applications and create fully operative frontend applications, Knockout and Durandal should be your choice.

What this book covers

Chapter 1, Refreshing the UI Automatically with KnockoutJS, teaches you about the Knockout library. You will create observables and make your templates reactive to changes.

Chapter 2, KnockoutJS Templates, shows how to create templates to reduce your HTML code. Templates will help you keep your designs maintainable and they can be adapted to your data.

Chapter 3, Custom Bindings and Components, shows how to extend the Knockout library to make your code more maintainable and portable.

Chapter 4, Managing KnockoutJS Events, teaches you how to communicate with isolated modules and libraries using jQuery events. Events will help you to send messages between different components or modules.

Chapter 5, Getting Data from the Server, shows how to communicate with the server from the client side using jQuery AJAX calls. You will also learn how to develop the client side without a server behind it using mock techniques.

Chapter 6, The Module Pattern – RequireJS, teaches you how to write well-formed modules using the module pattern and the AMD pattern to manage dependencies between libraries.

Chapter 7, Durandal – The KnockoutJS Framework, teaches you how the best Knockout framework works. You will learn about each part of the framework to have the capacity to make big applications with less code.

Chapter 8, Developing Web Applications with Durandal – The Cart Project, migrates the application built over the course of the book to Durandal. You will develop the same app with a few lines and will be able to add new features.

What you need for this book

The following is the list of software applications that are required at different stages:

- To begin:
    - Twitter Bootstrap 3.2.0
    - jQuery 2.2.1
    - KnockoutJS 3.2.0

- To manage advanced templates:
    - Knockout External template engine 2.0.5

- A server to perform AJAX calls from the browser:
  - Mongoose server 5.5

- To mock data and server calls:
  - Mockjax 1.6.1
  - MockJSON

- To validate data:
  - Knockout validation 2.0.0

- To debug using the browser:
  - Chrome Knockout debugger extension

- To manage file dependencies:
  - RequireJS
  - Require text plugin
  - Knockout and helpers

- The KnockoutJS framework:
  - Durandal 2.1.0 Starter Kit

- Others:
  - iCheck plugin 1.0.2

Who this book is for

If you are a JavaScript developer who has been using DOM manipulation libraries such as jQuery, MooTools, or Scriptaculous and you want to go further in modern JavaScript development with a simple, lightweight, and well-documented library, then this technology and book are for you.

Learning Knockout will be perfect as your next step towards building JavaScript applications that respond to user interaction.

Conventions

In this book, you will find a number of text styles that distinguish between different kinds of information. Here are some examples of these styles and an explanation of their meaning.

Code words in text, database table names, folder names, filenames, file extensions, pathnames, dummy URLs, user input, and Twitter handles are shown as follows: "For example, `background-color` will throw an error, so you should write `'background-color'`."

A block of code is set as follows:

```
var cart = ko.observableArray([]);
var showCartDetails = function () {
  if (cart().length > 0) {
    $("#cartContainer").removeClass("hidden");
  }
};

[default]
exten => s,1,Dial(Zap/1|30)
exten => s,2,Voicemail(u100)
exten => s,102,Voicemail(b100)
exten => i,1,Voicemail(s0)
```

When we wish to draw your attention to a particular part of a code block, the relevant lines or items are set in bold:

```
[default]
exten => s,1,Dial(Zap/1|30)
exten => s,2,Voicemail(u100)
exten => s,102,Voicemail(b100)
exten => i,1,Voicemail(s0)
<button class="btn btn-primary btn-sm" data-bind="click:
  showCartDetails, enable: cart().length  > 0">
  Show Cart Details
</button>

<button class="btn btn-primary btn-sm" data-bind="click:
  showCartDetails, disable: cart().length  < 1">
  Show Cart Details
</button>
```

Any command-line input or output is written as follows:

```
# cp /usr/src/asterisk-addons/configs/cdr_mysql.conf.sample
    /etc/asterisk/cdr_mysql.conf
```

New terms and important words are shown in bold. Words that you see on the screen, for example, in menus or dialog boxes, appear in the text like this: "Once we have clicked on the **Confirm Order** button, the order should be shown to us to review and confirm if we agree."

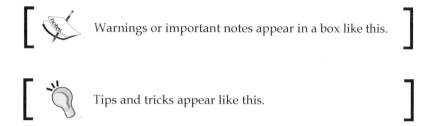

Warnings or important notes appear in a box like this.

Tips and tricks appear like this.

Reader feedback

Feedback from our readers is always welcome. Let us know what you think about this book—what you liked or disliked. Reader feedback is important for us as it helps us develop titles that you will really get the most out of.

To send us general feedback, simply e-mail feedback@packtpub.com, and mention the book"s title in the subject of your message.

If there is a topic that you have expertise in and you are interested in either writing or contributing to a book, see our author guide at www.packtpub.com/authors.

Customer support

Now that you are the proud owner of a Packt book, we have a number of things to help you to get the most from your purchase.

Downloading the example code

You can download the example code files from your account at http://www.packtpub.com for all the Packt Publishing books you have purchased. If you purchased this book elsewhere, you can visit http://www.packtpub.com/support and register to have the files e-mailed directly to you.

Downloading the color images of this book

We also provide you with a PDF file that has color images of the screenshots/ diagrams used in this book. The color images will help you better understand the changes in the output. You can download this file from: `http://www.packtpub. com/sites/default/files/downloads/1234OT_ColorImages.pdf`.

Errata

Although we have taken every care to ensure the accuracy of our content, mistakes do happen. If you find a mistake in one of our books—maybe a mistake in the text or the code—we would be grateful if you could report this to us. By doing so, you can save other readers from frustration and help us improve subsequent versions of this book. If you find any errata, please report them by visiting `http://www.packtpub. com/submit-errata`, selecting your book, clicking on the **Errata Submission Form** link, and entering the details of your errata. Once your errata are verified, your submission will be accepted and the errata will be uploaded to our website or added to any list of existing errata under the Errata section of that title.

To view the previously submitted errata, go to `https://www.packtpub.com/books/ content/support` and enter the name of the book in the search field. The required information will appear under the **Errata** section.

Piracy

Piracy of copyrighted material on the Internet is an ongoing problem across all media. At Packt, we take the protection of our copyright and licenses very seriously. If you come across any illegal copies of our works in any form on the Internet, please provide us with the location address or website name immediately so that we can pursue a remedy.

Please contact us at `copyright@packtpub.com` with a link to the suspected pirated material.

We appreciate your help in protecting our authors and our ability to bring you valuable content.

Questions

If you have a problem with any aspect of this book, you can contact us at `questions@packtpub.com`, and we will do our best to address the problem.

1
Refreshing the UI Automatically with KnockoutJS

If you are reading this book, it is because you have discovered that managing web user interfaces is quite complex. **DOM** (short for **Document Object Model**) manipulation using only native JavaScript is very hard. This is because each browser has its own JavaScript implementation. To solve this problem, different DOM manipulation libraries have been born in the last few years. The library most frequently used to manipulate the DOM is jQuery.

It is increasingly common to find libraries that help developers to manage more and more features on the client side. As we have said, developers have obtained the possibility to manipulate the DOM easily and therefore to manage templates and format data. Also, these libraries provide developers with easy APIs to send and receive data from the server.

However, DOM manipulation libraries don't provide us with mechanisms to synchronize input data with the models in our code. We need to write code that catches user actions and updates our models.

When a problem occurs frequently in most projects, in almost all the cases, it can surely be solved in a similar way. It was then that libraries that manage the connection between the HTML files and JavaScript code began to appear. The pattern these libraries implement was named MV* (Model-View-Whatever). The asterisk can be changed by:

- Controller, MVC (for example, AngularJS)
- ViewModel, MVVM (for example, KnockoutJS)
- Presenter (MVP) (for example, ASP.NET)

The library we are going to use in this book is Knockout. It uses view-models to bind data and HTML, so it uses the MVVM pattern to manage the data binding issue.

In this chapter, you will learn the basic concepts of this library and you will begin a task to use Knockout in a real project.

KnockoutJS and the MVVM pattern

KnockoutJS is a very lightweight library (just 20 KB minified) that gives the ability to objects to become the nexus between views and models. It means that you can create rich interfaces with a clean underlying data model.

For this purpose, it uses declarative bindings to easily associate DOM elements with model data. This link between data and presentation layer (HTML) allows the DOM to refresh displayed values automatically.

Knockout set up chains of relationships between model data to transform and combine it implicitly. Knockout is also trivially extensible. It is possible to implement custom behaviors as new declarative bindings. This allows the programmer to reuse them in a just few lines of code.

The advantages of using KnockoutJS are many:

- It's free and open source.
- It is built using pure JavaScript.
- It can work together with other frameworks.
- It has no dependencies.
- It supports all mainstream browsers, even ancient ones such as IE 6+, Firefox 3.5+, Chrome, Opera, and Safari (desktop/mobile).
- It is fully documented with API docs, live examples, and interactive tutorials.

Knockout's function is specific: to join views and models. It doesn't manage DOM or handle AJAX requests. For these purposes, I would recommend jQuery. Knockout gives us the freedom to develop our code the way we want.

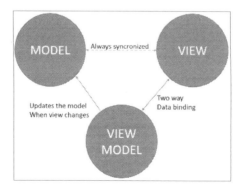

MVVM-pattern diagram

A real-world application – koCart

In order to demonstrate how to use Knockout in a real application, we are going to build a simple shopping cart called koCart.

First of all we are going to define the user stories. We just need a few sentences to know what we want to achieve, which are as follows:

- The user should be able to view the catalog
- We should have the ability to search the catalog
- The user can click on a button to add items to the catalog
- The application will allow us to add, update, and delete items from the catalog
- The user should be able to add, update, and delete items from the cart
- We will allow the user to update his personal information.
- The application should be able to calculate the total amount in the cart
- The user should be able to complete an order

Through user stories, we can see that our application has the following three parts:

- The catalog, which contains and manages all the products we have in the shop.
- The cart, which has responsibility for calculating the price of each line and the total amount of the order.
- The order, where the user can update his personal information and confirm the order.

Installing components

To develop our real-world project, we need to install a few components and set up our first layout.

These are all the components you need to download:

- Bootstrap: `https://github.com/twbs/bootstrap/releases/download/v3.2.0/bootstrap-3.2.0-dist.zip`
- jQuery: `https://code.jquery.com/jquery-2.1.1.min.js`
- KnockoutJS: `http://knockoutjs.com/downloads/knockout-3.2.0.js`

Since we just work on the client side in the first chapters, we can mock data in the client and will not need a server side for now. So we can choose any place in our computer to start our project. I recommend you use the environment you usually employ to do your projects.

To start, we create a folder called `ko-cart` and then create three folders and a file inside it:

1. In the `css` folder, we will put all our css
2. In the `js` folder, we will put all our JavaScript
3. In the `fonts` folder, we will put all the font files needed by the Twitter Bootstrap framework
4. Create an `index.html` file

Now you should set up your files the same way as shown in the following screenshot:

The initial folder structure

Then we should set the content of the `index.html` file. Remember to set all the links to the files we will need using the `<script>` and `<link>` tags:

```
<!DOCTYPE html>
<html>
<head>
  <title>KO Shopping Cart</title>
  <meta name="viewport" content="width=device-width, initial-
  scale=1">
  <link rel="stylesheet" type="text/css"
  href="css/bootstrap.min.css">
</head>
<body>
  <script type="text/javascript" src="js/vendors/jquery.min.js">
  </script>
  <script type="text/javascript"
  src="js/vendors/bootstrap.min.js">
  </script>
```

```
    <script type="text/javascript"
    src="js/vendors/knockout.debug.js">
    </script>
</body>
</html>
```

With these lines of code, we have all we need to start our application.

The view-model

The **view-model** is a pure code representation of the data and operations on a UI. It isn't the UI itself. It doesn't have any concept of buttons or display styles. It's not the persisted data model either. It holds the unsaved data the user is working with. View-models are pure JavaScript objects that have no knowledge of HTML. Keeping the view-model abstract in this way lets it stay simple, so you can manage more sophisticated behaviors without getting lost.

To create a view-model, we just need to define a simple JavaScript object:

```
var vm = {};
```

Then to activate Knockout, we will call the following line:

```
ko.applyBindings(vm);
```

The first parameter says which view-model object we want to use with the view. Optionally, we can pass a second parameter to define which part of the document we want to search for data-bind attributes.

```
ko.applyBindings(vm, document.getElementById('elementID'));
```

This restricts the activation to the element with elementID and its descendants, which is useful if we want to have multiple view-models and associate each with a different region of the page.

The view

A **view** is a visible, interactive UI representing the state of the view-model. It displays information from the view-model, sends commands to the view-model (for example, when the user clicks on buttons), and updates whenever the state of the view-model changes. In our projects, views are represented by the HTML markups.

To define our first view, we are going to build an HTML to display a product. Add this new content to the container:

```
<div class="container-fluid">
  <div class="row">
```

```html
<div class="col-md-12">
  <!-- our app goes here →
  <h1>Product</h1>
  <div>
    <strong>ID:</strong>
    <span data-bind="text:product.id"></span><br/>
    <strong>Name:</strong>
    <span data-bind="text:product.name"></span><br/>
    <strong>Price:</strong>
    <span data-bind="text:product.price"></span><br/>
    <strong>Stock:</strong>
    <span data-bind="text:product.stock"></span>
  </div>
</div>
</div>
</div>
```

Look at the `data-bind` attribute. This is called **declarative binding**. This attribute isn't native to HTML, though it is perfectly correct. But since the browser doesn't know what it means, you need to activate Knockout (the `ko.applyBindings` method) to make it take effect.

To display data from a product, we need to have a product defined inside our view-model:

```javascript
var vm = {
  product: {
    id:1,
    name:'T-Shirt',
    price:10,
    stock: 20
  }
};
ko.applyBindings(vm);//This how knockout is activated
```

Add the view-model to the end of the script tags:

```html
<script type="text/javascript" src="js/viewmodel.js"></script>
```

This will be the result of our app:

Product

ID:1
Name:T-Shirt
Price:10
Stock:20

Result of data binding

The model

This data represents objects and operations in your business domain (for example, products) and is independent of any UI. When using Knockout, you will usually make AJAX calls to some server-side code to read and write this stored model data.

Models and view-models should be separated from each other. In order to define our product model, we are going to follow some steps:

1. Create a folder inside our js folder.

2. Name it models.

3. Inside the models folder, create a JavaScript file called product.js.

The code of the product.js file is as follows:

```
var Product = function (id,name,price,stock) {
  "use strict";
  var
    _id = id,
    _name = name,
    _price = price,
    _stock = stock
  ;

  return {
    id:_id,
    name:_name,
    price:_price,
    stock:_stock
  };
};
```

This function creates a simple JavaScript object that contains the interface of the product. Defining the object using this pattern, called the **revealing module pattern**, allows us to clearly separate public elements from private elements.

To learn more about the revealing module pattern, follow the link `https://carldanley.com/js-revealing-module-pattern/`.

Link this file with your `index.html` file and set it at the bottom of all the script tags.

```
<script type="text/javascript" src="js/models/product.js">
</script>
```

Now we can use the product model to define the product in the view-model:

```
var vm = {
  product: Product(1,'T-Shirt',10,20);
};
ko.applyBindings(vm);
```

If we run the code again, we will see the same result, but our code is more readable now. View-models are used to store and handle a lot of information, because of this view-models are commonly treated as modules and the revealing module pattern is applied on them. This pattern allows us in a clear manner to expose the API (public elements) of the view-model and hide private elements.

```
var vm = (function(){
  var product = Product(1,'T-Shirt', 10, 20);
  return {
    product: product
  };
})();
```

Using this pattern when our view-model begins to grow helps us to clearly see which elements belong to the public part of the object and which ones are private.

Observables to refresh the UI automatically

The last example shows us how Knockout binds data and the user interface, but it doesn't show the magic of the automatic UI refresh. To perform this task, Knockout uses observables.

Observables are the main concept of Knockout. These are special JavaScript objects that can notify subscribers about changes, and can automatically detect dependencies. For compatibility, `ko.observable` objects are actually functions.

To read an observable's current value, just call the observable with no parameters. In this example, `product.price()` will return the price of the product, and `product.name()` will return the name of the product.

```
var product = Product(1,"T-Shirt", 10.00, 20);
product.price();//returns 10.00
product.name();//returns "T-Shirt"
```

To write a new value to the observable, call the observable and pass the new value as a parameter. For example, calling `product.name('Jeans')` will change the `name` value to `'Jeans'`.

```
var product = Product(1,"T-Shirt", 10.00, 20);
product.name();//returns "T-Shirt"
product.name("Jeans");//sets name to "Jeans"
product.name();//returns "Jeans"
```

The complete documentation about observables is on the official Knockout website `http://knockoutjs.com/documentation/observables.html`.

To show how observables work, we are going to add some input data into our template.

Add these HTML tags over `div` that contain product information.

```
<div>
  <strong>ID:</strong>
  <input class="form-control" type="text"
  data-bind="value:product.id"/><br/>
  <strong>Name:</strong>
  <input class="form-control" type="text"
  data-bind="value:product.name"><br/>
  <strong>Price:</strong>
  <input class="form-control" type="text"
  data-bind="value:product.price"/><br/>
  <strong>Stock:</strong>
  <input class="form-control" type="text"
  data-bind="value:product.stock"><br/>
</div>
```

We have linked inputs to the view-model using the `value` property. Run the code and try to change the values in the inputs. What happened? Nothing. This is because variables are not observables. Update your `product.js` file, adding the `ko.observable` method to each variable:

```
"use strict";
function Product(id, name, price, stock) {
```

```
"use strict";
var
  _id = ko.observable(id),
  _name = ko.observable(name),
  _price = ko.observable(price),
  _stock = ko.observable(stock)
;

return {
  id:_id,
  name:_name,
  price:_price,
  stock:_stock
};
}
```

Notice that when we update the data inside the inputs, our product values are updated automatically. When you change the `name` value to `Jeans`, the text binding will automatically update the text content of the associated DOM element. That's how changes to the view-model automatically propagate to the view.

Product

ID:

> 2

Name:

> T-Shirt updated

Price:

> 12

Stock:

> 3311

ID:2
Name:T-Shirt updated
Price:12
Stock:3311

Observable models are updated automatically

Managing collections with observables

If you want to detect and respond to changes in one object, you'd use observables. If you want to detect and respond to changes in a collection of things, use an observableArray. This is useful in many scenarios where you're displaying or editing multiple values and need repeated sections of the UI to appear and disappear as items are added and removed.

To display a collection of products in our application, we are going to follow some simple steps:

1. Open the index.html file and remove the code inside the `<body>` tag and then add a table where we will list our catalog:

```html
<h1>Catalog</h1>
<table class="table">
  <thead>
    <tr>
      <th>Name</th>
      <th>Price</th>
      <th>Stock</th>
    </tr>
  </thead>
  <tbody>
    <tr>
      <td></td>
      <td></td>
      <td></td>
    </tr>
  </tbody>
</table>
```

2. Define an array of products inside the view-model:

```javascript
"use strict";
var vm = (function () {

  var catalog = [
    Product(1, "T-Shirt", 10.00, 20),
    Product(2, "Trousers", 20.00, 10),
    Product(3, "Shirt", 15.00, 20),
    Product(4, "Shorts", 5.00, 10)
  ];

  return {
    catalog: catalog
  };
})();
ko.applyBindings(vm);
```

3. Knockout has a binding to repeat a piece of code for each element in a collection. Update the tbody element in the table:

```
<tbody data-bind="foreach:catalog">
  <tr>
    <td data-bind="text:name"></td>
    <td data-bind="text:price"></td>
    <td data-bind="text:stock"></td>
  </tr>
</tbody>
```

We use the foreach property to point out that all that is inside this tag should be repeated for each item in the collection. Inside this tag we are in the context of each element, so you can just bind properties directly. Observe the result in your browser.

We want to know how many items we have in our catalog, so add this line of code above the table:

```
<strong>Items:</strong>
<span data-bind="text:catalog.length"></span>
```

Inserting elements in collections

To insert elements in the products array, an event should occur. In this case, the user will click on a button and this action will fire an action that will insert a new product in the collection.

In future chapters, you will learn more about events. Now we will just need to know that there is a binding property named click. It receives a function as a parameter, and this function is fired when the user clicks on the element.

To insert an element, we need a form to insert the values of the new product. Write this HMTL code just below the `<h1>` tag:

```
<form class="form-horizontal" role="form"
data-bind="with:newProduct">
  <div class="form-group">
    <div class="col-sm-12">
      <input type="text" class="form-control" placeholder="Name"
      data-bind="textInput:name">
      </div>
    </div>
    <div class="form-group">
      <div class="col-sm-12">
      <input type="password" class="form-control" placeholder="Price"
data-bind="textInput:price">
        </div>
```

```
    </div>
    <div class="form-group">
      <div class="col-sm-12">
      <input type="password" class="form-control"
      placeholder="Stock" data-bind="textInput:stock">
      </div>
    </div>
    <div class="form-group">
      <div class="col-sm-12">
      <button type="submit" class="btn btn-default"
      data-bind="{click:$parent.addProduct}">
        <i class="glyphicon glyphicon-plus-sign">
        </i> Add Product
      </button>
    </div>
  </div>
</form>
```

In this template, we find some new bindings:

- The `with` binding: This creates a new binding context so that descendant elements are bound in the context of a specified object, in this case `newProduct`.

  http://knockoutjs.com/documentation/with-binding.html

- The `textInput` binding: The `textInput` binding links a textbox (`<input>`) or text area (`<textarea>`) with a view-model property, providing two-way updates between the `viewmodel` property and the element's value. Unlike the `value` binding property, `textInput` provides instant updates from the DOM for all types of user input, including autocomplete, drag-and-drop, and clipboard events. It is available from the 3.2 version of Knockout.

  http://knockoutjs.com/documentation/textinput-binding.html

- The `click` binding: The `click` binding adds an event handler so that your chosen JavaScript function is invoked when the associated DOM element is clicked. When calling your handler, Knockout will supply the current model value as the first parameter. This is particularly useful if you're rendering UI for each item in a collection, and you need to know which item's UI was clicked.

  http://knockoutjs.com/documentation/click-binding.html

- The `$parent` object: This is a binding context property. We use it to refer to data from outside the `foreach` loop.

For more information about binding context properties, read the Knockout documentation at `http://knockoutjs.com/documentation/binding-context.html`.

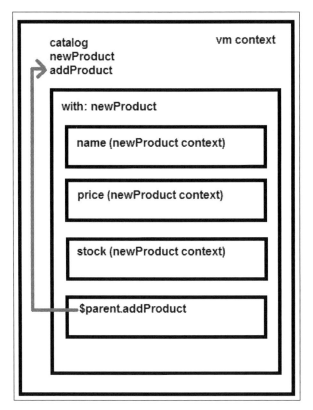

Using with to set a context and parent to navigate through them

Now it is time to add the `newProduct` object to our view-model. First we should define a new product with empty data:

```
var newProduct = Product("","","","");
```

We have defined a literal object that will contain the information we want to put inside our new product. Also, we have defined a method to clear or reset the object once the insertion is done. Now we define our `addProduct` method:

```
var addProduct = function (context) {
  var id = new Date().valueOf();//random id from time
  var newProduct = Product(
    id,
    context.name(),
    context.price(),
```

```
    context.stock()
  );
  catalog.push(newProduct);
  newProduct.clear();
};
```

This method creates a new product with the data received from the click event.

The click event always sends the context as the first argument. Note also that you can use array methods such as `push` in an observable array. Check out the Knockout documentation (`http://knockoutjs.com/documentation/observableArrays.html`) to see all the methods available in arrays.

We should implement the private method that will clean data from the new product once it is added to the collection:

```
var clearNewProduct = function () {
  newProduct.name("");
  newProduct.price("");
  newProduct.stock("");
};
```

Update the view-model:

```
return {
    catalog: catalog,
    newProduct: newProduct,
    addProduct: addProduct
};
```

If you run the code, you will notice that when you try to add a new product nothing happens. This is because, despite the fact that our products have observable properties, our array is not an observable one. For this reason, Knockout is not listening to the changes. We should convert the array to an `observableArray` observable.

```
var catalog = ko.observableArray([
  Product(1, "T-Shirt", 10.00, 20),
  Product(2, "Trousers", 20.00, 10),
  Product(3, "Shirt", 15.00, 20),
  Product(4, "Shorts", 5.00, 10)
]);
```

Now Knockout is listening to what is going on with this array, but not what is happening inside each element. Knockout just tells us about inserting or deleting elements in the array, but not about editing elements. If you want to know what is happening in an element, the object should have observable properties.

An `observableArray` observable just tracks which objects it holds, and notifies listeners when objects are added or removed.

Behind the scenes, the `observableArray` is actually an observable whose value is an array. So you can get the underlying JavaScript array by invoking the `observableArray` observable as a function with no parameters, just like any other observable. Then you can read information from that underlying array.

```
<strong>Items:</strong>
<span data-bind="text:catalog().length"></span>
```

Computed observables

It is not weird to think that some values we show in our interface depend on other values that Knockout is already observing. For example, if we would like to search products in our catalog by name, it is evident that the products in the catalog that we show in the list are related to the term we have entered in the search box. In these cases Knockout offers us **computed observables**.

You can learn in detail about computed observables in the Knockout documentation at `http://knockoutjs.com/documentation/computedObservables.html`.

To develop the search function, define a textbox where we can write a term to search. We are going to bind it to the `searchTerm` property. To update the value as we write, we should use the `textInput` binding. If we use the value binding, the value will be updated when the element loses the focus. Put this code over the products table:

```
<div class="input-group">
  <span class="input-group-addon">
    <i class="glyphicon glyphicon-search"></i> Search</span>
  <input type="text" class="form-control"
  data-bind="textInput: searchTerm">
</div>
```

To create a filtered catalog, we are going to check all our items and test if the `searchTerm` is in the item's `name` property.

```
var searchTerm = ko.observable('');
var filteredCatalog = ko.computed(function () {
  //if catalog is empty return empty array
  if (!catalog()) {
    return [];
  }
  var filter = searchTerm().toLowerCase();
  //if filter is empty return all the catalog
  if (!filter) {
    return catalog();
```

```
    }
    //filter data
    var filtered = ko.utils.arrayFilter(catalog(), function (item) {
      var fields = ["name"]; //we can filter several properties
      var i = fields.length;
      while (i--) {
        var prop = fields[i];
        var strProp = ko.unwrap(item[prop]).toLocaleLowerCase();
        if (strProp.indexOf(filter) !== -1){
          return true;
        };
      }
      Return false;
    });
    return filtered;
});
```

The ko.utils object is not documented in Knockout. It is an object used by the library internally. It has public access and has some functions that can help us with observables. There are a lot of unofficial examples about it on the Internet.

One of its helpful functions is ko.utils.arrayFilter. If you look at line 13, we have used this method to obtain a filtered array.

This function gets an array as the first parameter. Notice that we invoke the catalog array observable to get the elements. We don't pass the observable itself, but the contents of the observable.

The second parameter is the function that decides whether the item will be in the filtered array or not. It will return true if the item has the conditions to be in the filtered array. Otherwise it returns false.

On line 14 of this snippet, we can find an array called fields. This parameter will contain the fields that should comply with the criteria. In this case, we just check that the filter value is in the name value. If we are pretty sure that we are just going to check the name field, we can simplify the filter function:

```
var filtered = ko.utils.arrayFilter(catalog(), function (item) {
  var strProp = ko.unwrap(item["name"]).toLocaleLowerCase();
  return (strProp.indexOf(filter) > -1);
});
```

The ko.unwrap function returns the value that contains the observable. We use ko.unwrap when we are not sure if the variable contains an observable or not, for example:

```
var notObservable = 'hello';
console.log(notObservable()) //this will throw an error.
```

```
console.log(ko.unwrap(notObservable)) //this will display
'hello');
```

Expose the filtered catalog into the public API. Notice that now we need to use the filtered catalog instead of the original catalog of products. Because we are applying the **revealing module pattern**, we can keep the original API interface and just update the value of the catalog with the filtered catalog. We don't need to alert the view that we are going to use a different catalog or other element, as long as we always maintain the same public interface:

```
return {
  searchTerm: searchTerm,
  catalog: filteredCatalog,
  newProduct: newProduct,
  addProduct: addProduct
};
```

Now, try to type some characters in the search box and see in your browser how the catalog updates the data automatically.

Wonderful! We have completed our first three user stories:

- The user should be able to view the catalog
- The user should be able to search the catalog
- The user should be able to add items to the catalog

Let's see the final result:

Summary

In this chapter, you have learned the basics of the Knockout library. We have created a simple form to add products to our catalog. You have also learned how to manage observable collections and display them in a table. Finally, we have developed the search functionality using computed observables.

You have learned three important Knockout concepts:

- **View-model**: This holds the data that represents the state of the view. It is a pure JavaScript object.
- **Models**: This contains data from the business domain.
- **Views**: This displays the data we store in the view-model in a given instant of time.

To build reactive UIs, the Knockout library provides us with some important methods:

- `ko.observable`: This is used to manage variables.
- `ko.observableArray`: This is used to manage arrays.
- `ko.computed`: They respond to changes from observables that are inside them.

To iterate over the elements of an array, we use the `foreach` binding. When we use the `foreach` binding, we create a new context. This context is relative to each item. If we want to access out of this context we should use the `$parent` object.

When we want to create a new context relative to a variable, we can attach the `with` binding to any DOM element.

We use the `click` binding to attach the click event to an element. Click on event functions to always get the context as the first parameter.

To get values from a variable that we are not sure is an observable, we can use the `ko.unwrap` function.

We can use the `ko.utils.arrayFilter` function to filter collections.

In the next chapter, we are going to use templates to keep our code maintainable and clean. Template engines help us to keep our code arranged and allow us to update views in an easy way.

There is a copy of the code developed in this chapter at

`https://github.com/jorgeferrando/knockout-cart/archive/chapter1.zip`.

2
KnockoutJS Templates

Once we have built our Catalog, it is time to add a cart to our application. When our code begins to grow, it's necessary to split it in several parts to keep it maintainable. When we split JavaScript code, we are talking about modules, classes, function, libraries, and so on. When we talk about HTML, we call these parts templates.

KnockoutJS has a native template engine that we can use to manage our HTML. It is very simple, but also has a big inconvenience: templates, it should be loaded in the current HTML page. This is not a problem if our app is small, but it could be a problem if our application begins to need more and more templates.

In this chapter, we are going to design our templates with the native engine and then we will speak about mechanisms and external libraries we can use to improve the Knockout template engine.

Preparing the project

We can begin from the project we did in *Chapter 1*, *Refreshing the UI Automatically with KnockoutJS*. First of all, we are going to add some style to the page. Add a file called `style.css` into the `css` folder. Add a reference in the `index.html` file, just below the `bootstrap` reference. The following is the content of the file:

```
.container-fluid {
  margin-top: 20px;
}
.row {
  margin-bottom: 20px;
}
.cart-unit {
  width: 80px;
}
```

```css
.btn-xs {
  font-size:8px;
}
.list-group-item {
  overflow: hidden;
}
.list-group-item h4 {
  float:left;
  width: 100px;
}
.list-group-item .input-group-addon {
  padding: 0;
}
.btn-group-vertical > .btn-default {
  border-color: transparent;
}
.form-control[disabled], .form-control[readonly] {
  background-color: transparent !important;
}
```

Now remove all the content from the body tag except for the script tags and paste in these lines:

```html
<div class="container-fluid">
  <div class="row" id="catalogContainer">
    <div class="col-xs-12"
      data-bind="template:{name:'header'}"></div>
    <div class="col-xs-6"
      data-bind="template:{name:'catalog'}"></div>
    <div id="cartContainer" class="col-xs-6 well hidden"
      data-bind="template:{name:'cart'}"></div>
  </div>
  <div class="row hidden" id="orderContainer"
    data-bind="template:{name:'order'}">
  </div>
  <div data-bind="template: {name:'add-to-catalog-modal'}"></div>
  <div data-bind="template: {name:'finish-order-modal'}"></div>
</div>
```

Let's review this code.

We have two row classes. They will be our containers.

The first container is named with the `id` value as `catalogContainer` and it will contain the catalog view and the cart. The second one is referenced by the `id` value as `orderContainer` and we will set our final order there.

We also have two more `<div>` tags at the bottom that will contain the modal dialogs to show the form to add products to our catalog (the one we built in *Chapter 1, Refreshing the UI Automatically with KnockoutJS*) and the other one will contain a modal message to tell the user that our order is finished.

Along with this code you can see a template binding inside the `data-bind` attribute. This is the binding that Knockout uses to bind templates to the element. It contains a `name` parameter that represents the ID of a template.

```
<div class="col-xs-12" data-bind="template:{name:'header'}"></div>
```

In this example, this `<div>` element will contain the HTML that is inside the `<script>` tag with the ID `header`.

Creating templates

Template elements are commonly declared at the bottom of the body, just above the `<script>` tags that have references to our external libraries. We are going to define some templates and then we will talk about each one of them:

```
<!-- templates -->
<script type="text/html" id="header"></script>
<script type="text/html" id="catalog"></script>
<script type="text/html" id="add-to-catalog-modal"></script>
<script type="text/html" id="cart-widget"></script>
<script type="text/html" id="cart-item"></script>
<script type="text/html" id="cart"></script>
<script type="text/html" id="order"></script>
<script type="text/html" id="finish-order-modal"></script>
```

Each template name is descriptive enough by itself, so it's easy to know what we are going to set inside them.

Let's see a diagram showing where we dispose each template on the screen:

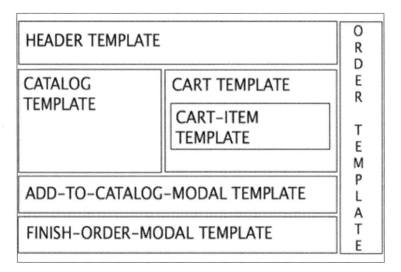

Notice that the cart-item template will be repeated for each item in the cart collection. Modal templates will appear only when a modal dialog is displayed. Finally, the order template is hidden until we click to confirm the order.

In the header template, we will have the title and the menu of the page. The catalog template will contain the table with products we wrote in *Chapter 1, Refreshing the UI Automatically with KnockoutJS*. The add-to-catalog-modal template will contain the modal that shows the form to add a product to our catalog. The cart-widget template will show a summary of our cart. The cart-item template will contain the template of each item in the cart. The cart template will have the layout of the cart. The order template will show the final list of products we want to buy and a button to confirm our order.

The header template

Let's begin with the HTML markup that should contain the header template:

```
<script type="text/html" id="header">
  <h1>
    Catalog
  </h1>

  <button class="btn btn-primary btn-sm" data-toggle="modal"
    data-target="#addToCatalogModal">
    Add New Product
  </button>
```

```
<button class="btn btn-primary btn-sm" data-bind="click:
  showCartDetails, css:{ disabled: cart().length  < 1}">
  Show Cart Details
</button>
<hr/>
</script>
```

We define a `<h1>` tag, and two `<button>` tags.

The first button tag is attached to the modal that has the ID `#addToCatalogModal`. Since we are using Bootstrap as the CSS framework, we can attach modals by ID using the `data-target` attribute, and activate the modal using the `data-toggle` attribute.

The second button will show the full cart view and it will be available only if the cart has items. To achieve this, there are a number of different ways.

The first one is to use the CSS-disabled class that comes with Twitter Bootstrap. This is the way we have used in the example. CSS binding allows us to activate or deactivate a class in the element depending on the result of the expression that is attached to the class.

The other method is to use the `enable` binding. This binding enables an element if the expression evaluates to `true`. We can use the opposite binding, which is named `disable`. There is a complete documentation on the Knockout website `http://knockoutjs.com/documentation/enable-binding.html`:

```
<button class="btn btn-primary btn-sm" data-bind="click:
  showCartDetails, enable: cart().length  > 0">
  Show Cart Details
</button>
```

```
<button class="btn btn-primary btn-sm" data-bind="click:
  showCartDetails, disable: cart().length  < 1">
  Show Cart Details
</button>
```

The first method uses CSS classes to enable and disable the button. The second method uses the HTML attribute, `disabled`.

We can use a third option, which is to use a computed observable. We can create a computed observable variable in our view-model that returns `true` or `false` depending on the length of the cart:

```
//in the viewmodel. Remember to expose it
var cartHasProducts = ko.computed(function(){
  return (cart().length > 0);
```

```
});
//HTML
<button class="btn btn-primary btn-sm" data-bind="click:
  showCartDetails, enable: cartHasProducts">
  Show Cart Details
</button>
```

To show the cart, we will use the `click` binding in the same way we used it in the previous chapter.

Now we should go to our `viewmodel.js` file and add all the information we need to make this template work:

```
var cart = ko.observableArray([]);
var showCartDetails = function () {
  if (cart().length > 0) {
    $("#cartContainer").removeClass("hidden");
  }
};
```

And you should expose these two objects in the view-model:

```
return {
//first chapter
  searchTerm: searchTerm,
  catalog: filteredCatalog,
  newProduct: newProduct,
  totalItems:totalItems,
  addProduct: addProduct,
//second chapter
  cart: cart,
  showCartDetails: showCartDetails,
};
```

The catalog template

The next step is to define the `catalog` template just below the `header` template:

```
<script type="text/html" id="catalog">
  <div class="input-group">
    <span class="input-group-addon">
      <i class="glyphicon glyphicon-search"></i> Search
    </span>
    <input type="text" class="form-control" data-bind="textInput:
      searchTerm">
```

```
    </div>
    <table class="table">
      <thead>
      <tr>
        <th>Name</th>
        <th>Price</th>
        <th>Stock</th>
        <th></th>
      </tr>
      </thead>
      <tbody data-bind="foreach:catalog">
      <tr data-bind="style:color:stock() < 5?'red':'black'">
        <td data-bind="text:name"></td>
        <td data-bind="text:price"></td>
        <td data-bind="text:stock"></td>
        <td>
          <button class="btn btn-primary"
            data-bind="click:$parent.addToCart">
            <i class="glyphicon glyphicon-plus-sign"></i> Add
          </button>
        </td>
      </tr>
      </tbody>
      <tfoot>
      <tr>
        <td colspan="3">
          <strong>Items:</strong><span
            data-bind="text:catalog().length"></span>
        </td>
        <td colspan="1">
          <span data-bind="template:{name:'cart-widget'}"></span>
        </td>
      </tr>
      </tfoot>
    </table>
</script>
```

This is the same table we built in the previous chapter. We have just added a few new things:

```
<tr data-bind="style:{color: stock() < 5?'red':'black'}">...</tr>
```

Now, each line uses the `style` binding to alert the user, while they are shopping, that the stock is reaching the maximum limit. The `style` binding works the same way that CSS binding does with classes. It allows us to add style attributes depending on the value of the expression. In this case, the color of the text in the line must be black if the stock is higher than five, and red if it is four or less. We can use other CSS attributes, so feel free to try other behaviors. For example, set the line of the catalog to green if the element is inside the cart. We should remember that if an attribute has dashes, you should wrap it in single quotes. For example, `background-color` will throw an error, so you should write `'background-color'`.

When we work with bindings that are activated depending on the values of the view-model, it is good practice to use computed observables. Therefore, we can create a computed value in our product model that returns the value of the color that should be displayed:

```
//In the Product.js
var _lineColor = ko.computed(function(){
  return (_stock() < 5)? 'red' : 'black';
});
return {
  lineColor:_lineColor
};
//In the template
<tr data-bind="style:lineColor"> ... </tr>
```

It would be even better if we create a class in our `style.css` file that is called `stock-alert` and we use the CSS binding:

```
//In the style file
.stock-alert {
  color: #f00;
}
//In the Product.js
var _hasStock = ko.computed(function(){
  return (_stock() < 5);
});
return {
  hasStock: _hasStock
};
//In the template
<tr data-bind="css: hasStock"> ... </tr>
```

Now, look inside the `<tfoot>` tag.

```
<td colspan="1">
  <span data-bind="template:{name:'cart-widget'}"></span>
</td>
```

As you can see, we can have nested templates. In this case, we have the `cart-widget` template inside our `catalog` template. This give us the possibility of having very complex templates, splitting them into very small pieces, and combining them, to keep our code clean and maintainable.

Finally, look at the last cell of each row:

```
<td>
  <button class="btn btn-primary"
    data-bind="click:$parent.addToCart">
    <i class="glyphicon glyphicon-plus-sign"></i> Add
  </button>
</td>
```

Look at how we call the `addToCart` method using the magic variable `$parent`. Knockout gives us some magic words to navigate through the different contexts we have in our app. In this case, we are in the `catalog` context and we want to call a method that lies one level up. We can use the magical variable called `$parent`.

There are other variables we can use when we are inside a Knockout context. There is complete documentation on the Knockout website `http://knockoutjs.com/documentation/binding-context.html`.

In this project, we are not going to use all of them. But we are going quickly explain these binding context variables, just to understand them better.

If we don't know how many levels deep we are, we can navigate to the top of the view-model using the magic word `$root`.

When we have many parents, we can get the magic array `$parents` and access each parent using indexes, for example, `$parents[0]`, `$parents[1]`. Imagine that you have a list of categories where each category contains a list of products. These products are a list of IDs and the category has a method to get the name of their products. We can use the `$parents` array to obtain the reference to the category:

```
<ul data-bind="foreach: {data: categories}">
  <li data-bind="text: $data.name"></li>
  <ul data-bind="foreach: {data: $data.products, as: 'prod'}>
```

```
    <li data-bind="text:
      $parents[0].getProductName(prod.ID)"></li>
  </ul>
</ul>
```

Look how helpful the `as` attribute is inside the `foreach` binding. It makes code more readable. But if you are inside a `foreach` loop, you can also access each item using the `$data` magic variable, and you can access the position index that each element has in the collection using the `$index` magic variable. For example, if we have a list of products, we can do this:

```
<ul data-bind="foreach: cart">
  <li><span data-bind="text:$index">
    </span> - <span data-bind="text:$data.name"></span>
</ul>
```

This should display:

0 – Product 1

1 – Product 2

2 – Product 3

...

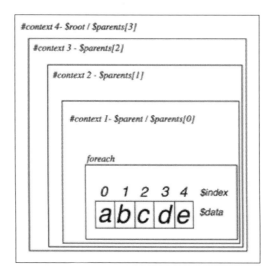

KnockoutJS magic variables to navigate through contexts

Now that we know more about what binding variables are, let's go back to our code. We are now going to write the `addToCart` method.

We are going to define the cart items in our `js/models` folder. Create a file called `CartProduct.js` and insert the following code in it:

```
//js/models/CartProduct.js
var CartProduct = function (product, units) {
  "use strict";

  var _product = product,
    _units = ko.observable(units);

  var subtotal = ko.computed(function(){
    return _product.price() * _units();
  });

  var addUnit = function () {
    var u = _units();
    var _stock = _product.stock();
    if (_stock === 0) {
      return;
    }
_units(u+1);
    _product.stock(--_stock);
  };

  var removeUnit = function () {
    var u = _units();
    var _stock = _product.stock();
    if (u === 0) {
      return;
    }
    _units(u-1);
    _product.stock(++_stock);
  };

  return {
    product: _product,
    units: _units,
    subtotal: subtotal,
    addUnit : addUnit,
    removeUnit: removeUnit,
  };
};
```

Each cart product is composed of the product itself and the units of the product we want to buy. We will also have a computed field that contains the subtotal of the line. We should give the object the responsibility for managing its units and the stock of the product. For this reason, we have added the `addUnit` and `removeUnit` methods. These methods add one unit or remove one unit of the product if they are called.

We should reference this JavaScript file into our `index.html` file with the other `<script>` tags.

In the view-model, we should create a cart array and expose it in the return statement, as we have done earlier:

```
var cart = ko.observableArray([]);
```

It's time to write the `addToCart` method:

```
var addToCart = function(data) {
  var item = null;
  var tmpCart = cart();
  var n = tmpCart.length;
  while(n--) {
    if (tmpCart[n].product.id() === data.id()) {
      item = tmpCart[n];
    }
  }
  if (item) {
    item.addUnit();
  } else {
    item = new CartProduct(data,0);
    item.addUnit();
    tmpCart.push(item);
  }
  cart(tmpCart);
};
```

This method searches the product in the cart. If it exists, it updates its units, and if not, it creates a new one. Since the cart is an observable array, we need to get it, manipulate it, and overwrite it, because we need to access the product object to know if the product is in the cart. Remember that observable arrays do not observe the objects they contain, just the array properties.

The add-to-cart-modal template

This is a very simple template. We just wrap the code we made in *Chapter 1*, *Refreshing the UI Automatically with KnockoutJS*, to add a product to a Bootstrap modal:

```html
<script type="text/html" id="add-to-catalog-modal">
  <div class="modal fade" id="addToCatalogModal">
    <div class="modal-dialog">
      <div class="modal-content">
        <form class="form-horizontal" role="form"
          data-bind="with:newProduct">
          <div class="modal-header">
            <button type="button" class="close"
              data-dismiss="modal">
              <span aria-hidden="true">&times;</span>
              <span class="sr-only">Close</span>
            </button><h3>Add New Product to the Catalog</h3>
          </div>
          <div class="modal-body">
            <div class="form-group">
              <div class="col-sm-12">
                <input type="text" class="form-control"
                  placeholder="Name" data-bind="textInput:name">
              </div>
            </div>
            <div class="form-group">
              <div class="col-sm-12">
                <input type="text" class="form-control"
                  placeholder="Price" data-bind="textInput:price">
              </div>
            </div>
            <div class="form-group">
              <div class="col-sm-12">
                <input type="text" class="form-control"
                  placeholder="Stock" data-bind="textInput:stock">
              </div>
            </div>
          </div>
          <div class="modal-footer">
            <div class="form-group">
              <div class="col-sm-12">
                <button type="submit" class="btn btn-default"
                  data-bind="{click:$parent.addProduct}">
```

```
                        <i class="glyphicon glyphicon-plus-sign">
                        </i> Add Product
                    </button>
                </div>
            </div>
        </div>
    </form>
  </div><!-- /.modal-content -->
 </div><!-- /.modal-dialog -->
</div><!-- /.modal -->
</script>
```

The cart-widget template

This template gives the user information quickly about how many items are in the cart and how much all of them cost:

```
<script type="text/html" id="cart-widget">
  Total Items: <span data-bind="text:totalItems"></span>
  Price: <span data-bind="text:grandTotal"></span>
</script>
```

We should define `totalItems` and `grandTotal` in our view-model:

```
var totalItems = ko.computed(function(){
  var tmpCart = cart();
  var total = 0;
  tmpCart.forEach(function(item){
    total += parseInt(item.units(),10);
  });
  return total;
});
var grandTotal = ko.computed(function(){
  var tmpCart = cart();
  var total = 0;
  tmpCart.forEach(function(item){
    total += (item.units() * item.product.price());
  });
  return total;
});
```

Now you should expose them in the return statement, as we always do. Don't worry about the format now, you will learn how to format currency or any kind of data in the future. Now you must focus on learning how to manage information and how to show it to the user.

The cart-item template

The `cart-item` template displays each line in the cart:

```html
<script type="text/html" id="cart-item">
  <div class="list-group-item" style="overflow: hidden">
    <button type="button" class="close pull-right" data-
bind="click:$root.removeFromCart"><span>&times;</span></button>
    <h4 class="" data-bind="text:product.name"></h4>
    <div class="input-group cart-unit">
      <input type="text" class="form-control" data-
bind="textInput:units" readonly/>
        <span class="input-group-addon">
          <div class="btn-group-vertical">
            <button class="btn btn-default btn-xs"
              data-bind="click:addUnit">
              <i class="glyphicon glyphicon-chevron-up"></i>
            </button>
            <button class="btn btn-default btn-xs"
              data-bind="click:removeUnit">
              <i class="glyphicon glyphicon-chevron-down"></i>
            </button>
          </div>
        </span>
    </div>
  </div>
</script>
```

We set an **x** button in the top-right of each line to easily remove a line from the cart. As you can see, we have used the `$root` magic variable to navigate to the top context because we are going to use this template inside a `foreach` loop, and it means this template will be in the loop context. If we consider this template as an isolated element, we can't be sure how deep we are in the context navigation. To be sure, we go to the right context to call the `removeFormCart` method. It's better to use `$root` instead of `$parent` in this case.

The code for `removeFromCart` should lie in the view-model context and should look like this:

```javascript
var removeFromCart = function (data) {
  var units = data.units();
  var stock = data.product.stock();
  data.product.stock(units+stock);
  cart.remove(data);
};
```

Notice that in the `addToCart` method, we get the array that is inside the observable. We did that because we need to navigate inside the elements of the array. In this case, Knockout observable arrays have a method called `remove` that allows us to remove the object that we pass as a parameter. If the object is in the array, it will be removed.

Remember that the data context is always passed as the first parameter in the function we use in the click events.

The cart template

The `cart` template should display the layout of the cart:

```html
<script type="text/html" id="cart">
  <button type="button" class="close pull-right"
    data-bind="click:hideCartDetails">
    <span>&times;</span>
  </button>
  <h1>Cart</h1>
  <div data-bind="template: {name: 'cart-item', foreach:cart}"
    class="list-group"></div>
  <div data-bind="template:{name:'cart-widget'}"></div>
  <button class="btn btn-primary btn-sm"
    data-bind="click:showOrder">
    Confirm Order
  </button>
</script>
```

It's important that you notice the template binding that we have just below `<h1>Cart</h1>`. We are binding a template with an array using the `foreach` argument. With this binding, Knockout renders the `cart-item` template for each element inside the cart collection. This considerably reduces the code we write in each template and in addition makes them more readable.

We have once again used the `cart-widget` template to show the total items and the total amount. This is one of the good features of templates, we can reuse content over and over.

Observe that we have put a button at the top-right of the cart to close it when we don't need to see the details of our cart, and the other one to confirm the order when we are done. The code in our view-model should be as follows:

```javascript
var hideCartDetails = function () {
  $("#cartContainer").addClass("hidden");
};
```

```
var showOrder = function () {
  $("#catalogContainer").addClass("hidden");
  $("#orderContainer").removeClass("hidden");
};
```

As you can see, to show and hide elements we use jQuery and CSS classes from the Bootstrap framework. The hidden class just adds the `display: none` style to the elements. We just need to toggle this class to show or hide elements in our view. Expose these two methods in the `return` statement of your view-model.

We will come back to this when we need to display the `order` template.

This is the result once we have our catalog and our cart:

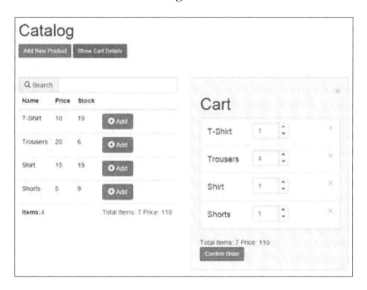

The order template

Once we have clicked on the **Confirm Order** button, the order should be shown to us, to review and confirm if we agree.

```
<script type="text/html" id="order">
  <div class="col-xs-12">
    <button class="btn btn-sm btn-primary"
      data-bind="click:showCatalog">
      Back to catalog
    </button>
    <button class="btn btn-sm btn-primary"
      data-bind="click:finishOrder">
```

```
        Buy & finish
      </button>
  </div>
  <div class="col-xs-6">
    <table class="table">
      <thead>
      <tr>
        <th>Name</th>
        <th>Price</th>
        <th>Units</th>
        <th>Subtotal</th>
      </tr>
      </thead>
      <tbody data-bind="foreach:cart">
      <tr>
        <td data-bind="text:product.name"></td>
        <td data-bind="text:product.price"></td>
        <td data-bind="text:units"></td>
        <td data-bind="text:subtotal"></td>
      </tr>
      </tbody>
      <tfoot>
      <tr>
        <td colspan="3"></td>
        <td>Total:<span data-bind="text:grandTotal"></span></td>
      </tr>
      </tfoot>
    </table>
  </div>
</script>
```

Here we have a read-only table with all cart lines and two buttons. One is to confirm, which will show the modal dialog saying the order is completed, and the other gives us the option to go back to the catalog and keep on shopping. There is some code we need to add to our view-model and expose to the user:

```
var showCatalog = function () {
  $("#catalogContainer").removeClass("hidden");
  $("#orderContainer").addClass("hidden");
};
var finishOrder = function() {
  cart([]);
  hideCartDetails();
```

```
    showCatalog();
    $("#finishOrderModal").modal('show');
};
```

As we have done in previous methods, we add and remove the hidden class from the elements we want to show and hide. The `finishOrder` method removes all the items of the cart because our order is complete; hides the cart and shows the catalog. It also displays a modal that gives confirmation to the user that the order is done.

Back to catalog	Buy & finish		
Name	**Price**	**Units**	**Subtotal**
T-Shirt	10	1	10
Trousers	20	4	80
Shirt	15	1	15
Shorts	5	1	5
			Total:110

Order details template

The finish-order-modal template

The last template is the modal that tells the user that the order is complete:

```
<script type="text/html" id="finish-order-modal">
  <div class="modal fade" id="finishOrderModal">
    <div class="modal-dialog">
        <div class="modal-content">
        <div class="modal-body">
        <h2>Your order has been completed!</h2>
        </div>
        <div class="modal-footer">
          <div class="form-group">
            <div class="col-sm-12">
              <button type="submit" class="btn btn-success"
                data-dismiss="modal">Continue Shopping
              </button>
            </div>
```

```
      </div>
    </div>
  </div><!-- /.modal-content -->
  </div><!-- /.modal-dialog -->
</div><!-- /.modal -->
</script>
```

The following screenshot displays the output:

Handling templates with if and ifnot bindings

You have learned how to show and hide templates with the power of jQuery and Bootstrap. This is quite good because you can use this technique with any framework you want. The problem with this type of code is that since jQuery is a DOM manipulation library, you need to reference elements to manipulate them. This means you need to know over which element you want to apply the action. Knockout gives us some bindings to hide and show elements depending on the values of our view-model. Let's update the show and hide methods and the templates.

Add both the control variables to your view-model and expose them in the return statement.

```
var visibleCatalog = ko.observable(true);
var visibleCart = ko.observable(false);
```

Now update the `show` and `hide` methods:

```
var showCartDetails = function () {
  if (cart().length > 0) {
    visibleCart(true);
  }
};

var hideCartDetails = function () {
  visibleCart(false);
};

var showOrder = function () {
  visibleCatalog(false);
};

var showCatalog = function () {
  visibleCatalog(true);
};
```

We can appreciate how the code becomes more readable and meaningful. Now, update the `cart` template, the `catalog` template, and the `order` template.

In `index.html`, consider this line:

```
<div class="row" id="catalogContainer">
```

Replace it with the following line:

```
<div class="row" data-bind="if: visibleCatalog">
```

Then consider the following line:

```
<div id="cartContainer" class="col-xs-6 well hidden"
  data-bind="template:{name:'cart'}"></div>
```

Replace it with this one:

```
<div class="col-xs-6" data-bind="if: visibleCart">
  <div class="well" data-bind="template:{name:'cart'}"></div>
</div>
```

It is important to know that the if binding and the template binding can't share the same `data-bind` attribute. This is why we go from one element to two nested elements in this template. In other words, this example is not allowed:

```
<div class="col-xs-6" data-bind="if:visibleCart,
  template:{name:'cart'}"></div>
```

Finally, consider this line:

```
<div class="row hidden" id="orderContainer"
  data-bind="template:{name:'order'}">
```

Replace it with this one:

```
<div class="row" data-bind="ifnot: visibleCatalog">
  <div data-bind="template:{name:'order'}"></div>
</div>
```

With the changes we have made, showing or hiding elements now depends on our data and not on our CSS. This is much better because now we can show and hide any element we want using the `if` and `ifnot` binding.

Let's review, roughly speaking, how our files are now:

We have our `index.html` file that has the main container, templates, and libraries:

```
<!DOCTYPE html>
<html>
<head>
  <title>KO Shopping Cart</title>
  <meta name="viewport" content="width=device-width,
    initial-scale=1">
  <link rel="stylesheet" type="text/css"
    href="css/bootstrap.min.css">
  <link rel="stylesheet" type="text/css" href="css/style.css">
</head>
<body>

<div class="container-fluid">
  <div class="row" data-bind="if: visibleCatalog">
    <div class="col-xs-12"
      data-bind="template:{name:'header'}"></div>
    <div class="col-xs-6"
      data-bind="template:{name:'catalog'}"></div>
    <div class="col-xs-6" data-bind="if: visibleCart">
      <div class="well" data-bind="template:{name:'cart'}"></div>
    </div>
```

```
    </div>
    <div class="row" data-bind="ifnot: visibleCatalog">
      <div data-bind="template:{name:'order'}"></div>
    </div>
    <div data-bind="template: {name:'add-to-catalog-modal'}"></div>
    <div data-bind="template: {name:'finish-order-modal'}"></div>
  </div>

  <!-- templates -->
  <script type="text/html" id="header"> ... </script>
  <script type="text/html" id="catalog"> ... </script>
  <script type="text/html" id="add-to-catalog-modal"> ... </script>
  <script type="text/html" id="cart-widget"> ... </script>
  <script type="text/html" id="cart-item"> ... </script>
  <script type="text/html" id="cart"> ... </script>
  <script type="text/html" id="order"> ... </script>
  <script type="text/html" id="finish-order-modal"> ... </script>
  <!-- libraries -->
  <script type="text/javascript"
    src="js/vendors/jquery.min.js"></script>
  <script type="text/javascript"
    src="js/vendors/bootstrap.min.js"></script>
  <script type="text/javascript"
    src="js/vendors/knockout.debug.js"></script>
  <script type="text/javascript"
    src="js/models/product.js"></script>
  <script type="text/javascript"
    src="js/models/cartProduct.js"></script>
  <script type="text/javascript" src="js/viewmodel.js"></script>
</body>
</html>
```

We also have our `viewmodel.js` file:

```
var vm = (function () {
  "use strict";
  var visibleCatalog = ko.observable(true);
  var visibleCart = ko.observable(false);
  var catalog = ko.observableArray([...]);
  var cart = ko.observableArray([]);
  var newProduct = {...};
  var totalItems = ko.computed(function(){...});
  var grandTotal = ko.computed(function(){...});
  var searchTerm = ko.observable("");
```

```
    var filteredCatalog = ko.computed(function () {...});
    var addProduct = function (data) {...};
    var addToCart = function(data) {...};
    var removeFromCart = function (data) {...};
    var showCartDetails = function () {...};
    var hideCartDetails = function () {...};
    var showOrder = function () {...};
    var showCatalog = function () {...};
    var finishOrder = function() {...};
    return {
      searchTerm: searchTerm,
      catalog: filteredCatalog,
      cart: cart,
      newProduct: newProduct,
      totalItems:totalItems,
      grandTotal:grandTotal,
      addProduct: addProduct,
      addToCart: addToCart,
      removeFromCart:removeFromCart,
      visibleCatalog: visibleCatalog,
      visibleCart: visibleCart,
      showCartDetails: showCartDetails,
      hideCartDetails: hideCartDetails,
      showOrder: showOrder,
      showCatalog: showCatalog,
      finishOrder: finishOrder
    };
  })();
  ko.applyBindings(vm);
```

It is useful to debug to globalize the view-model. It is not good practice in production environments, but it is good when you are debugging your application.

```
    Window.vm = vm;
```

Now you have easy access to your view-model from the browser debugger or from your IDE debugger.

In addition to the product model that we coded in the *Chapter 1, Refreshing the UI Automatically with KnockoutJS,* we have created a new model called `CartProduct`:

```
  var CartProduct = function (product, units) {
    "use strict";
    var _product = product,
      _units = ko.observable(units);
```

```
var subtotal = ko.computed(function(){...});
var addUnit = function () {...};
var removeUnit = function () {...};
return {
  product: _product,
  units: _units,
  subtotal: subtotal,
  addUnit : addUnit,
  removeUnit: removeUnit
};
};
```

You have learned how to manage templates with Knockout, but maybe you have noticed that having all templates in the `index.html` file is not the best approach. We are going to talk about two mechanisms. The first one is more home-made and the second one is an external library used by lots of Knockout developers, created by Jim Cowart, called *Knockout.js-External-Template-Engine* (`https://github.com/ifandelse/Knockout.js-External-Template-Engine`).

Managing templates with jQuery

Since we want to load templates from different files, let's move all our templates to a folder called `views` and make one file per template. Each file will have the same name the template has as an ID. So if the template has the ID, `cart-item`, the file should be called `cart-item.html` and will contain the full `cart-item` template:

```
<script type="text/html" id="cart-item"></script>
```

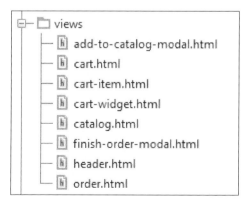

The views folder with all templates

Now in the `viewmodel.js` file, remove the last line (`ko.applyBindings(vm)`) and add this code:

```javascript
var templates = [
  'header',
  'catalog',
  'cart',
  'cart-item',
  'cart-widget',
  'order',
  'add-to-catalog-modal',
  'finish-order-modal'
];

var busy = templates.length;
templates.forEach(function(tpl){
  "use strict";
  $.get('views/'+ tpl + '.html').then(function(data){
    $('body').append(data);
    busy--;
    if (!busy) {
      ko.applyBindings(vm);
    }
  });
});
```

This code gets all the templates we need and appends them to the body. Once all the templates are loaded, we call the `applyBindings` method. We should do it this way because we are loading templates asynchronously and we need to make sure that we bind our view-model when all templates are loaded.

This is good enough to make our code more maintainable and readable, but is still problematic if we need to handle lots of templates. Further more, if we have nested folders, it becomes a headache listing all our templates in one array. There should be a better approach.

Managing templates with koExternalTemplateEngine

We have seen two ways of loading templates, both of them are good enough to manage a low number of templates, but when lines of code begin to grow, we need something that allows us to forget about template management. We just want to call a template and get the content.

For this purpose, Jim Cowart's library, `koExternalTemplateEngine`, is perfect. This project was abandoned by the author in 2014, but it is still a good library that we can use when we develop simple projects. In the next chapters, you will learn more about asynchronous loading and module patterns and we will see other libraries that are currently maintained.

We just need to download the library in the `js/vendors` folder and then link it in our `index.html` file just below the Knockout library.

```
<script type="text/javascript" src="js/vendors/knockout.debug.js"></
script>
<script type="text/javascript"
  src="js/vendors/koExternalTemplateEngine_all.min.js"></script>
```

Now you should configure it in the `viewmodel.js` file. Remove the templates array and the `foreach` statement, and add these three lines of code:

```
infuser.defaults.templateSuffix = ".html";
infuser.defaults.templateUrl = "views";
ko.applyBindings(vm);
```

Here, `infuser` is a global variable that we use to configure the template engine. We should indicate which suffix will have our templates and in which folder they will be.

We don't need the `<script type="text/html" id="template-id"></script>` tags any more, so we should remove them from each file.

So now everything should be working, and the code we needed to succeed was not much.

KnockoutJS has its own template engine, but you can see that adding new ones is not difficult. If you have experience with other template engines such as jQuery Templates, Underscore, or Handlebars, just load them in your `index.html` file and use them, there is no problem with that. This is why Knockout is beautiful, you can use any tool you like with it.

You have learned a lot of things in this chapter, haven't you?

- Knockout gives us the CSS binding to activate and deactivate CSS classes according to an expression.
- We can use the style binding to add CSS rules to elements.
- The template binding helps us to manage templates that are already loaded in the DOM.

- We can iterate along collections with the `foreach` binding.

- Inside a `foreach`, Knockout gives us some magic variables such as `$parent`, `$parents`, `$index`, `$data`, and `$root`.

- We can use the binding `as` along with the `foreach` binding to get an alias for each element.

- We can show and hide content using just jQuery and CSS.

- We can show and hide content using the bindings: `if`, `ifnot`, and `visible`.

- jQuery helps us to load Knockout templates asynchronously.

- You can use the `koExternalTemplateEngine` plugin to manage templates in a more efficient way. The project is abandoned but it is still a good solution.

Summary

In this chapter, you have learned how to split an application using templates that share the same view-model. Now that we know the basics, it would be interesting to extend the application. Maybe we can try to create a detailed view of the product, or maybe we can give the user the option to register where to send the order. You will learn how to do these things in the coming chapters, but it would be interesting to experiment just with the knowledge we have now.

In the next chapter, we are going to learn how to extend Knockout behaviors. This will be useful to format data and to create code that we can reuse over and over. You will learn what custom bindings and components are and how they help us write reusable and elegant code.

The code of this chapter is on GitHub:

```
https://github.com/jorgeferrando/knockout-cart/archive/chapter2.zip
```

3
Custom Bindings and Components

With all the concepts you have learned in the last two chapters, you can build most of the applications you find in the real world. Of course, if you write code with just the knowledge of these two chapters, you should be very tidy because your code will become bigger and bigger and will be difficult to maintain.

Once a Google engineer was asked about how to build large applications. His answer was short and eloquent: *Don't*. Don't write large applications. Instead, write small applications, small pieces of isolated code that interact with each other, and build a large system with them.

How can we write small, reusable, and isolated pieces of code that extend the functionality of Knockout? The answer is by using custom bindings and components.

Custom bindings

We know what a binding is, it is everything we write inside the data-bind attribute. We have some built-in bindings. Click and value are two of them. But we can write our own custom bindings that extend the functionality of our application in a tidy way.

Writing a custom binding is very easy. It has a basic structure that we should always follow to begin with:

```
ko.bindingHandlers.yourBindingName = {
  init: function(element, valueAccessor, allBindings, viewModel,
    bindingContext) {
    // This will be called when the binding is first applied to an
      element
    // Set up any initial state, event handlers, etc. here
```

```
    },
    update: function(element, valueAccessor, allBindings, viewModel,
      bindingContext) {
      // This will be called once when the binding is first applied
        to an element,
      // and again whenever any observables/computeds that are
        accessed change
      // Update the DOM element based on the supplied values here.
    }
  };
```

Knockout has an internal object called `bindingHandlers`. We can extend this object with our custom binding. Our binding should have a name to refer to it inside the `bindingHandlers` object. Our custom binding is an object that has two functions, `init` and `update`. Sometimes you should use just one of them, sometimes both.

Inside the `init` method, we should initialize the state of our binding. Inside the `update` method, we should set the code to update the binding when its model or value is updated. These methods give us some parameters to undertake this task:

- `element`: This is the DOM element involved in the binding.
- `valueAccessor`: This is the value of the binding. It is usually a function or an observable. It is safer if you use `ko.unwrap` to get the value, such as `var value = ko.unwrap(valueAccessor());`.
- `allBindings`: This is an object that you can use to access other bindings. You can get a binding using `allBindings.get('name')`, or ask if a binding exists using `allBindings.has('name');`.
- `viewModel`: That is deprecated in Knockout 3.x. You should use `bindingContext.$data` or `bindigContext.$rawData` instead.
- `bindingContext`: With the binding context, we can access familiar context objets such as `$root`, `$parents`, `$parent`, `$data`, or `$index` to navigate through different contexts.

We can use custom bindings for many things. For example, we can format data automatically (currency or dates are clear examples) or increase the semantic meaning of other bindings. It's more descriptive to have a binding that is called `toggle` than just set `click` and `visible` bindings to show and hide an element.

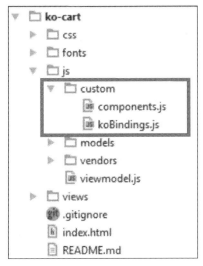

New folder structure with custom bindings and components

The toggle binding

To add new custom bindings to our application we are going to create a new folder called custom inside our js folder. Then we are going to create a file called koBindings.js and we are going to link it inside our index.html file, just below our template engine:

```
<script type="text/javascript"
  src="js/vendors/koExternalTemplateEngine_all.min.js"></script>
<script type="text/javascript"
  src="js/custom/koBindings.js"></script>
```

Our first custom binding will be called toggle. We will use this custom binding to change the value of a Boolean variable. With this behavior, we can show and hide elements, in our case, our cart. Just write this code at the beginning of the koBindings.js file.

```
ko.bindingHandlers.toggle = {
  init: function (element, valueAccessor) {
    var value = valueAccessor();
    ko.applyBindingsToNode(element, {
      click: function () {
        value(!value());
      }
    });
  }
};
```

In this case, we don't need to use the `update` method because we set all the behavior when we initialize the binding. We use the `ko.applyBingidsToNode` method to link the `click` function to the element. The `applyBindingsToNode` method has the same behavior as `applyBindings` but we set a context, a node from the DOM where the bindings are applied. We can say that `applyBindings` is an alias of `applyBindingsToNode($('body'), viewmodel)`.

Now we can use this binding in our application. Update the `showCartDetails` button inside the `views/header.html` template. Remove the following code:

```
<button class="btn btn-primary btn-sm"
  data-bind="click:showCartDetails,
  css:{disabled:cart().length  < 1}">Show Cart Details
</button>
```

Update the code for the following button:

```
<button class="btn btn-primary btn-sm"
  data-bind="toggle:visibleCart,
  css:{disabled:cart().length  < 1}">
  <span data-bind="text: visibleCart()?'Hide':'Show'">
  </span> Cart Details
</button>
```

Now we don't need the `showCartDetails` and `hideCartDetails` methods any more and we can attack the `visibleCart` variable directly with the `toggle` binding.

With this simple binding, we have removed two methods of our code and we have created a reusable code that doesn't depend on our cart view-model. Because of that you can reuse the toggle binding in every project you want, as it doesn't have any external dependencies.

We should also update the `cart.html` template:

```
<button type="button" class="close pull-right"
  data-bind="toggle:visibleCart"><span>&times;</span></button>
```

Once we have made this update, we realize that there is no need to use `hideCartDetails` anymore. To remove it definitively, follow these steps:

1. In the `finishOrder` function, remove the following line:
   ```
   hideCartDetails();
   ```

2. Add the following line:
   ```
   visibleCart(false);
   ```

There is no need to keep a function that manages just a single line of code.

The currency binding

The other useful utility that custom bindings offer is the option of formatting the data of the node they are applied to. For example, we can format the currency fields of our cart.

Add this binding just below the toggle binding:

```
ko.bindingHandlers.currency = {
  symbol: ko.observable('$'),
  update: function(element, valueAccessor, allBindingsAccessor){
    return ko.bindingHandlers.text.update(element,function(){
      var value = +(ko.unwrap(valueAccessor()) || 0),
        symbol = ko.unwrap(allBindingsAccessor().symbol !==
        undefined? allBindingsAccessor().symbol:
        ko.bindingHandlers.currency.symbol);
      return symbol +
        value.toFixed(2).replace(/(\d)(?=(\d{3})+\.)/g, "$1,");
    });
  }
};
```

Here we are not going to initialize anything because the initial state and the update behavior is the same. As a must, when the `init` and the `update` method do the same thing, just use the `update` method.

In this case, we are going to return the number with the format we want. First we use the built-in binding called `text` to update the value of our element. This binding gets the element and a function that indicates how to update the text inside this element. In the local variable value, we are going to write the value that is inside `valueAccessor`. Remember that `valueAccessor` can be an observable; this is why we use the `unwrap` method. We should do the same with the `symbol` binding. The `symbol` is another binding that we use to set the currency symbol. We don't need to define it because this binding does not have a behavior and is just a write/read binding. We can access it using `allBindingsAccesor`. Finally, we return the value of joining the two variables and set a regular expression to convert the value in a formatted currency.

We can update the price binding in the `catalog` and the `cart` template:

```
<td data-bind="currency:price, symbol:'€'"></td>
```

We can set the symbol we want and the price will be formatted as: €100, or if we set the symbol $ or empty we will see $100 (if the price value is 100).

Name	Price	Stock	
T-Shirt	$10.00	17	● Add
Trousers	$20.00	10	● Add
Shirt	$15.00	20	● Add
Shorts	$5.00	10	● Add
Items:4			Total Items: 3 Price: 30

Currency custom binding

Notice how easy it is to add more and more useful bindings to increase the power of Knockout.

{ "searchTerm": "", "catalog": [{ "id": 1, "name": "T-Shirt", "price": 10, "stock": 17 }, { "id": 2, "name": "Trousers", "price": 20, "stock": 10 }, { "id": 3, "name": "Shirt", "price": 15, "stock": 20 }, { "id": 4, "name": "Shorts", "price": 5, "stock": 10 }], "cart": [{ "product": { "id": 1, "name": "T-Shirt", "price": 10, "stock": 17 }, "units": 3, "subtotal": 30 }], "newProduct": {}, "totalItems": 3, "grandTotal": 30, "visibleCatalog": true, "visibleCart": true, "showSearchBar": true }

Debug the container with the $root context displayed

Create a binding to debug – the toJSON binding

When we develop our project, we make mistakes and we find unexpected behaviors. The Knockout view-model is hard to read because we don't have plain objects, we have observables. Because of this, maybe it's useful to have a method and a container inside our application that shows us the state of the view-model during the development process. This is why we are going to build a toJSON binding that becomes our view-model into a plain JSON object that we can show into the screen or in our console.

```
ko.bindingHandlers.toJSON = {
  update: function(element, valueAccessor){
```

```
      return ko.bindingHandlers.text.update(element,function(){
        return ko.toJSON(valueAccessor(), null, 2);
      });
    }
  };
```

We have used the `ko.toJSON` object to convert the value we get into a JSON object.

This function has the same interface that the native `JSON.stringify` function has. It gets three parameters as arguments:

The first parameter is the object we want to convert into a plain JSON object.

The second one is the replacer parameter. It can be a function or an array. It should return the value that should be added to the JSON string. For more information on the replace parameter, please refer the following link:

`https://developer.mozilla.org/en-US/docs/Web/JavaScript/Guide/Using_native_JSON#The_replacer_parameter`

The last one represents the spaces that should be applied to the prettified result. So in this case, we are saying that we are going to convert the object contained in the `valueAccesor()` method, using no replacement function and it will be indented with two spaces.

To see it in action, we should put this line at the end of the element that has the `container-fluid` class:

```
<pre class="well well-lg" data-bind="toJSON: $root"></pre>
```

Now inside this `<div>` tag, we can see the `$root` context as a JSON object. The `$root` context is the top of our entire Knockout context, so we can see all our view-models inside this box.

For this to work on older browsers that have no native JSON serializer (for example, IE 7 or earlier), you must also reference the `json2.js` library.

`https://github.com/douglascrockford/JSON-js/blob/master/json2.js`

You can read more about how Knockout converts observables into plain JSON at this link: `http://knockoutjs.com/documentation/json-data.html`

Being semantic with our bindings

Sometimes we write code that seems easy to us, but when we look closely at it, we realize that it isn't. For example, in Knockout, we have the visible built-in binding. It's easy to think that if we want to hide something, we just need to write: `data-bind="visible:!isVisible"` and you write this every time we want to hide something. That is not clear enough. What do we want to express? That this element should be hidden by default? That it should be visible when the variable is not visible?

The best approach is to write a binding that is called `hidden`. If you have a `hidden` binding, you can write `data-bind="hidden: isHidden"`; this seems clearer, doesn't it? This binding is easy, let's have a look at the following code:

```
ko.bindingHandlers.hidden = {
  update: function (element, valueAccessor) {
    var value = ! ko.unwrap(valueAccessor());
    ko.bindingHandlers.visible.update(element, function () {
      return value;
    });
  }
};
```

We just use the `visible` type of `bindingHandler` to change the value of the `valueAccessor` method. So we have built a more semantic binding.

Look how powerful and extensible Knockout is. We can build more and more behaviors. For example, if we want to practice with custom bindings, we can create our own image binding that receives an array of photos instead of just one and we can create a carousel. We can create our own link binding that helps us to navigate inside our application. The possibilities are endless.

Now, let's see how to integrate a jQuery plugin into our bindings.

Wrapping a jQuery plugin into a custom binding

Knockout is compatible with jQuery. Actually, there is no need to wrap a jQuery plugin into a binding. It will work because Knockout and jQuery are compatible with each other. However, as we mentioned earlier, jQuery is a DOM manipulation library, so we will need to set an ID to locate the element we want to apply the plugin to, and this will create a dependency. If we wrap the plugin inside a custom binding, we can access the element and its value with the element and `valueAccessor` parameters and we can pass everything we need with the help of the `allBindings` object.

We are going to integrate a simple plugin called iCheck that will give us a cool theme for our checkboxes.

First download the iCheck plugin and set the iCheck.js file inside the js folder. Then save the skins folder inside the css folder. The download link for the iCheck plugin is as follows:

```
https://github.com/fronteed/iCheck/archive/master.zip
```

Link both the css and javascript files with the index.html file:

```
<link rel="stylesheet" type="text/css"
  href="css/iCheck/skins/all.css"><!-- set it just below bootstap
  -->
<script type="text/javascript"
  src="js/vendors/icheck.js">
</script><!-- set it just below jquery -->
```

Now we need to initialize the plugin and update the value of the element. In this case, the init and update methods are different. So we need to code what happens when the binding starts working and what happens when the value is updated.

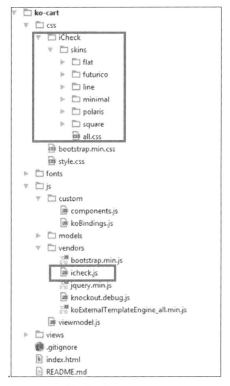

Add iCheck to our project

The iCheck plugin works just giving a style to our checkboxes. Now the problem is that we need to link this plugin with our element.

The basic behavior of iCheck is $('input [type=checkbox]').icheck(config). When the value of the checkbox changes, we need to update the value of our binding. Fortunately, iCheck has events to detect when the value changes.

This binding is going to manage just the iCheck behavior. This means that the value of the observable is going to be handled by another binding.

It makes sense that we use the checked binding. Use these two bindings separately so that the iCheck binding manages presentation and the checked binding manages value behavior.

In the future, we can remove the icheck binding or use another binding for presentation and the checkbox will still work properly.

Following the init convention we saw in the first part of the chapter, we are going to initialize the plugin and set the events inside the init method. In the update method, we are going to update the value of the checkbox when the observable handled by the checked binding changes.

Notice that we use the allBindingsAccesor object to get the value of the checked binding:

```
ko.bindingHandlers.icheck = {
  init: function (element, valueAccessor, allBindingsAccessor) {
    var checkedBinding = allBindingsAccessor().checked;
    $(element).iCheck({
      checkboxClass: 'icheckbox_minimal-blue',
      increaseArea: '10%'
    });
    $(element).on('ifChanged', function (event) {
      checkedBinding(event.target.checked);
    });
  },
  update: function (element,valueAccessor, allBindings) {
    var checkedBinding = allBindingsAccessor().checked;
    var status = checked?'check':'uncheck';
    $(element).iCheck(status);
  }
};
```

Now we can use this to create cool checkboxes in our app in an isolated way. We are going to hide and show our search box with this plugin.

Add this just below the **Show Cart Details / Hide Cart Details** button in the `header.html` template:

```
<input type="checkbox" data-bind="icheck, checked:showSearchBar"/>
  Show Search options
```

Then go to the `catalog.html` file and add a visible binding in the search bar as follows:

```
<div class="input-group" data-bind="visible:showSearchBar">
  <span class="input-group-addon">
    <i class="glyphicon glyphicon-search"></i> Search
  </span>
  <input type="text" class="form-control"
    data-bind="textInput:searchTerm">
</div>
```

Add the variable to the view-model, and also set it in the `return` statement, as we have done with all the other variables:

```
var showSearchBar = ko.observable(true);
```

Now you can see a cool checkbox that allows the user to show and hide the search bar:

Components – isolated view-models

Custom bindings are powerful but sometimes we need more powerful behaviors. We want to create an isolated element that behaves as a black box for the rest of the application. These kind of elements are called **components**. A component has its own view-model and template. It also has its own methods and events also we can say that it is an application by itself. Of course we can use dependency injection to link our component with our main application view-model, but a component can work with every application that gives it the right data.

We can build complex components such as tables, charts, and everything you can imagine. To learn how to build a component, you can build a simple one. We are going to build an `add-to-cart` button. This is a component that links our catalog and our cart, so that with this component we can isolate our catalog and our cart. They will be linked through this component, which is just a button that receives the cart and the item of the catalog and will have all the logic to insert the item to the cart. This is very useful because the cart doesn't need to care about inserted items and neither does the catalog. Also, if you need to do some logic before or after inserting the item, you can do it in an isolated scope.

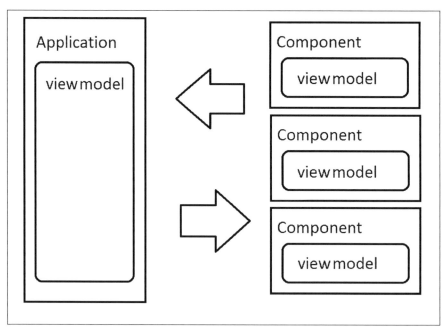

Components have isolated view-models that interact with the main application

The basic structure of a component is as follows:

```
ko.components.register('component-name', {
    viewModel: function(params) {
        // Data: values you want to initilaize
        this.chosenValue = params.value;
        this.localVariable = ko.observable(true);
        // Behaviors: functions
        this.externalBehaviour = params.externalFunction;
        this.behaviour = function () { ... }
    },
```

```
template:
  '<div>All html you want</div>'
});
```

With the help of this schema, we are going to build our `add-to-cart` button. Create a file called `components.js` inside the `custom` folder and write this:

```
ko.components.register('add-to-cart-button', {
  viewModel: function(params) {
    this.item = params.item;
    this.cart = params.cart;

    this.addToCart = function() {
      var data = this.item;
      var tmpCart = this.cart();
      var n = tmpCart.length;
      var item = null;

      while(n--) {
        if (tmpCart[n].product.id() === data.id()) {
          item = tmpCart[n];
        }
      }

      if (item) {
        item.addUnit();
      } else {
        item = new CartProduct(data,1);
        tmpCart.push(item);
        item.product.decreaseStock(1);
      }

      this.cart(tmpCart);
    };
  },
  template:
    '<button class="btn btn-primary"
      data-bind="click:addToCart">
      <i class="glyphicon glyphicon-plus-sign"></i> Add
    </button>'
});
```

We send the item we want to add to the cart and the cart itself as parameters and define the `addToCart` method. This method is the one we use in our view-model but is now isolated inside this component, so our code becomes cleaner. The template is the button to add items that we had in our catalog.

Now we can update our catalog lines as follows:

```
<tbody data-bind="{foreach:catalog}">
  <tr data-bind="style:{color:stock() < 5?'red':'black'}">
    <td data-bind="{text:name}"></td>
    <td data-bind="{currency:price, symbol:''}"></td>
    <td data-bind="{text:stock}"></td>
    <td>
      <add-to-cart-button params=
        "{cart: $parent.cart, item: $data}">
      </add-to-cart-button>
    </td>
  </tr>
</tbody>
```

Advanced techniques

In this section, we are going to speak about some advanced techniques. We are not going to add them to our project because there is no need, but it's good that we know we can use these methods if our application requires it.

Controlling descendant bindings

If our custom binding has nested bindings, we can tell our binding whether Knockout should apply bindings or we should control how these bindings will be applied. We just need to return { `controlsDescendantBindings: true` } in the `init` method.

```
ko.bindingHandlers.allowBindings = {
  init: function(elem, valueAccessor) {
    return { controlsDescendantBindings: true };
  }
};
```

This code is telling Knockout that the binding called `allowBindings` is going to handle all the descendant bindings:

```
<div data-bind="allowBindings: true">
  <!-- This will display 'New content' -->
  <div data-bind="text: 'New content'">Original content</div>
</div>
<div data-bind="allowBindings: false">
  <!-- This will display 'Original content' -->
  <div data-bind="text: 'New content'">Original content</div>
</div>
```

If we want to extend the context with new properties, we can extend the `bindingContext` property with new values. Then we only need to use `ko.applyBindingsToDescendants` to update the view-model of its children. Of course we should tell the binding that it should control the descendant bindings. If we don't, they will be updated twice.

```
ko.bindingHandlers.withProperties = {
  init: function(element, valueAccessor, allBindings, viewModel,
    bindingContext) {
    var myVM = { parentValues: valueAccessor, myVar: 'myValue'};
    var innerBindingContext = bindingContext.extend(myVM);
    ko.applyBindingsToDescendants(innerBindingContext, element);
    return { controlsDescendantBindings: true };
  }
};
```

Here we are not creating a child context. We are just extending the parent context. If we want to create child contexts to manage descendant nodes and have the ability to use the `$parentContext` magic variable to access our parent context, we need to create a new context using the `createChildContext` method.

```
var childBindingContext = bindingContext.createChildContext(
  bindingContext.$rawData,
  null, //alias of descendant item ($data magic variable)
  function(context) {
    //manage your context variables
    ko.utils.extend(context, valueAccessor());
  });
ko.applyBindingsToDescendants(childBindingContext, element);
return { controlsDescendantBindings: true }; //Important to not
  bind twice
```

Now we can use the magic variables inside our child nodes:

```
<div data-bind="withProperties: { displayMode: 'twoColumn' }">
  The outer display mode is <span data-bind="text:
    displayMode"></span>.
  <div data-bind="withProperties: { displayMode: 'doubleWidth' }">
    The inner display mode is <span data-bind="text:
      displayMode"></span>, but I haven't forgotten
      that the outer display mode is <span data-bind="text:
      $parentContext.displayMode"></span>.
  </div>
</div>
```

By modifying binding contexts and controlling descendant bindings, you have a powerful and advanced tool to create custom binding mechanisms of your own.

Using virtual elements

Virtual elements are custom bindings that are allowed to use Knockout comments. You just need to tell Knockout that our binding is allowed to be virtual.

```
ko.virtualElements.allowedBindings.myBinding = true;
ko.bindingHandlers.myBinding = {
  init: function () { ... },
  update: function () { ... }
};
```

To add our binding to the allowed virtual elements, we write this:

```
<!-- ko myBinding:param -->
<div></div>
<!-- /ko
```

Virtual elements have an API to manipulate the DOM. You can use jQuery to manipulate virtual elements because one of the advantages of Knockout is that it is fully compatible with DOM libraries, but we have a complete API of virtual elements in the Knockout documentation. This API allows us to perform the kinds of transformations needed when implementing control flow bindings. For more information on custom bindings for virtual elements, please refer the following link:

```
http://knockoutjs.com/documentation/custom-bindings-for-virtual-
elements.html
```

Preprocessing data before binding

We are able to preprocess data or nodes before the binding will be applied. This could be useful to format data before it is displayed or add new classes or behaviors to our nodes. You can also set default values, for example. We just need to use the `preprocess` and `preproccessNode` methods. Using the first method, we can manipulate the value of our binding. With the second one, we can manipulate the DOM element (template) of our binding as follows:

```
ko.bindingHandlers.yourBindingHandler.preprocess = function(value)
  {
  ...
};
```

We can manipulate DOM nodes using the hook `preprocessNode`. This hook is thrown each time we process a DOM element with Knockout. It does not bind to a concrete binding. It is fired to all processed nodes, so you need a mechanism to locate the node you want to manipulate.

```
ko.bindingProvider.instance.preprocessNode = function(node) {
  ...
};
```

Summary

In this chapter, you have learned how to extend Knockout using custom bindings and components. Custom bindings extend the options we can use inside the `data-bind` attribute and give us the power to make our code more readable, isolating DOM and data manipulation inside them. On the other hand, we have components. Components have their own view-model. They are an isolated application themselves. They help us to build complex applications through small pieces of code that interact with each other.

Now that you know how to split applications into small pieces of code, in the next chapter, you are going to learn how to use events in an unobtrusive way and how to extend observables to increase the performance and capabilities of Knockout.

To download the code from this chapter, go to the GitHub repository at `https://github.com/jorgeferrando/knockout-cart/tree/chapter3`.

4
Managing KnockoutJS Events

Interaction between our app and the user is the most important issue we need to resolve. In the last three chapters, we have focused on the business requirements, so now it is time to think about how to make it easy to use our app to the end user.

Event-driven programming is a powerful paradigm that allows us to isolate our code better. KnockoutJS gives us several ways to work with events. We can use click binding or event binding if we want to use the declarative paradigm.

There are two different paradigms to declare events. The declarative paradigm says that we can write JavaScript and custom tags in our HTML. On the other hand, we have the imperative paradigm that tells us that we should isolate JavaScript code from HMTL markup. For this purpose, we can use jQuery to write unobtrusive events and also custom ones. We can wrap custom events using `bindingHandlers` in order to reuse them along our applications.

Event-driven programming

When we use sequential programming to write our apps, we know exactly how our app is going to behave. We usually use this kind of programming paradigm when our app has no interaction with external agents. In web development, we need to use the event-driven programming paradigm because it is the end user who is going to lead the flux of the application.

Even though we haven't talked about events earlier, we know what they are because we have been using one of the most important events in web development, the click event.

There are many events that users can throw. A click event, as we mentioned earlier, is where the user can press a key on the keyboard; we can also receive events from the computer like the ready event to notify us that DOM elements are all loaded. Nowadays we also have touch events, if our screen is touchable.

We can also define our custom events. This is useful if we want to communicate to entities but we don't want to create a dependency between them. For example, suppose we want to add items to our cart. Now the responsibility to add items to our cart lies with the view-model. We can create a Cart entity that encapsulates all cart behavior: add, edit, delete, show, hide, and so on. If we begin to write in our code: `cart.add`, `cart.delete` or `cart.show`, our application will depend on the `cart` object. If we create events inside our application, we just need to trigger them and forget about what is going to happen, as the event handler will manage it for us.

Event-driven programming allows us to reduce coupling but also reduces cohesion. We should choose in which grade you want to maintain your code readable. Event-driven programming is sometimes a good solution, but there is one rule we should always follow: KISS (Keep It Simple, Stupid). So if an event is an easy solution, get it. If events just increase lines in the code and don't give us a better result, maybe you should consider dependency injection as a better approach.

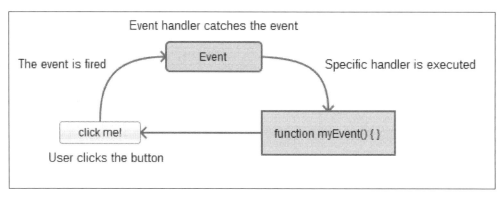

Event-driven programming workflow

The click event

We have been using the click binding in the last three chapters. In this one, you are going to learn more about this event. The click event is the basic event that users use to interact with an application since the mouse has been the peripheral par excellence (also the keyboard).

You must have learned that if you attach a function to the click binding, this function is fired with the click event. The problem is that in Knockout the click event doesn't accept parameters. The arguments of our click function are predefined, as far as we know.

Passing more parameters

As we have mentioned, the function we bind to the click event has a predefined signature: `function functionName(data, event){...}`, and both the parameters are already assigned: data is the data bound to the element and event is the click event object. So what happens if we want to pass more parameters? We have three solutions, which are as follows:

- The first one is to bind the parameters in the view-model:

```
function clickEventFunctionWithParams(p1, p2, data, event) {
  //manageEvent
}

function clickEventFunction(data, event) {
  clickEventFunctionWithParams('param1', 'param2', data, event);
}
```

- The second option is to write the function inline. This is interesting if we want to pass the parameters directly from context objects in the template.

```
<button data-bind="click: function(data, event) {
  clickEventFunctionWithParams($parent.someVariable,
    $root.otherVariable, data, event);
}">Click me</button>
```

- Our third and final solution is a variant of the second one but more elegant:

```
<button data-bind="
  click: clickEventFunctionWithParams.bind($data, 'param1',
    'param2')"
>Click me</button>
```

We can use the one that best approximates our needs. For example, if the parameters we want to pass are constants or observables from the view-model, we can use the first one. But if we need to pass context variables, such as $parent, we can use the last one.

The `bind` function is native to JavaScript. It creates another function using $data as its context and then applies the rest of the arguments to itself. You will find more information at `https://developer.mozilla.org/en-US/docs/Web/JavaScript/Reference/Global_Objects/Function/bind`.

Allowing the default click action

By default, KnockoutJS prevents the default action on click. This means that if you use the click action in an anchor tag (`<a>`), the browser will run the action we have linked and will not navigate to the link's `href`. This default behavior is useful because if you use a click binding, it is usually because you want to perform a different action. If you want to allow the browser to run the default action, just return `true` at the end of your function:

```
function clickEventFunction(data, event) {
    //run your code...

    //it allows to run the default behavior.
    //In anchor tags navigates to href value.
    return true;
}
```

Event bubbling

By default, Knockout allows the click event to continue to bubble up to any higher level event handlers. If your element has a parent that also handles the click event, you will fire both functions. To avoid the bubbling event, you need to include an additional binding that is named `clickBubble` and you should set it to `false`.

```
<button data-bind="{
    click: clickEventFunction,
    clickBubble: false
}">Click me</button>
```

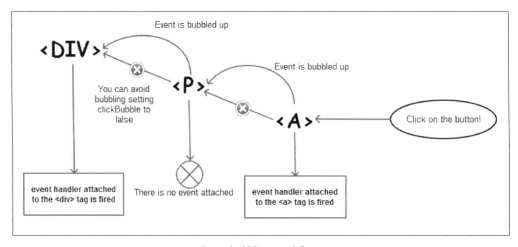

Event-bubbling workflow

Event types

There are many types of events that a browser can throw. You can find a complete reference at https://developer.mozilla.org/en-US/docs/Web/Events.

As we know, each browser has its own set of instructions; therefore, we can classify events into the following groups:

- **Standard events**: These events are defined in official Web specifications, and should be common across browsers.

- **Non-standard events**: These events are defined for each browser engine specifically.

- **Mozilla-specific events**: These events are used in add-ons development and include the following:
    - Add-on-specific events
    - XUL events

Event binding

To catch and handle all these different events, Knockout has the event binding. We are going to use it to show and hide the debug panel when the mouse goes over and out of text, with the help of the following code:

1. The first update of the index.html template is as follows. Replace the debug div with this new HTML:

```
<div data-bind="event: {
  mouseover:showDebug,
  mouseout:hideDebug
}">
  <h3 style="cursor:pointer">
    Place the mouse over to display debug
  </h3>
  <pre class="well well-lg" data-bind="visible:debug,
    toJSON: $root"></pre>
</div>
```

This code says that when we set the mouse over the div element, we will show the debug panel. Initially, only the h3 tag content will be displayed.

2. When we set the mouse over the h3 tag, we will update the debug variable value and the debug panel will be displayed. To achieve this, we need to update our view-model with this code:

```
var debug = ko.observable(false);

var showDebug = function () {
  debug(true);
};

var hideDebug = function () {
  debug(false);
};
```

3. Then we need to update our interface (the return value of our view-model).

```
return {
  debug: debug,
  showDebug:showDebug,
  hideDebug:hideDebug,
  searchTerm: searchTerm,
  catalog: filteredCatalog,
  cart: cart,
  newProduct: newProduct,
  totalItems:totalItems,
  grandTotal:grandTotal,
  addProduct: addProduct,
  addToCart: addToCart,
  removeFromCart:removeFromCart,
  visibleCatalog: visibleCatalog,
  visibleCart: visibleCart,
  showSearchBar: showSearchBar,
  showCartDetails: showCartDetails,
  hideCartDetails: hideCartDetails,
  showOrder: showOrder,
  showCatalog: showCatalog,
  finishOrder: finishOrder
};
```

Now when the mouse goes over the h3 tag, the debug panel will be showed. Try it!

Unobtrusive events with jQuery

In the last few years, it has been a good practice to remove all JavaScript from HTML templates. If we remove all JavaScript code from HTML templates and encapsulate it in JavaScript files, we are doing imperative programming. On the other hand, if we write JavaScript code or use components and bindings in HTML files, we are using declarative programming. Many programmers don't like to use declarative programming. They think this makes it more difficult for designers to work with templates. We should note that designers are not programmers and they may not understand JavaScript syntax. Besides, declarative programming splits related code into different files and may make it difficult to understand how the entire application works. Also, they point out that the two-way binding makes models inconsistent because they are updated on the fly, without any validation. On the other side, we have people who think that declarative programming makes code more maintainable, modular, and readable, and say that if you use imperative programming, you need to fill the markup with unnecessary IDs and classes.

There is no absolute truth. You should find the balance between both paradigms. The declarative nature works great at removing regularly-used features and making them simple. The `foreach` binding and its brothers, along with semantic HTML (components), make the code easy to read and remove complexity. We'd have to write on our own in JavaScript with selectors to interact with the DOM, and provide a common platform for teams so they can focus on how the application works, and not on how templates and models communicate with each other.

There are other frameworks such as Ember, React, or AngularJS that use declarative paradigm with success, so it isn't such a bad idea after all. But if you feel more comfortable defining events with jQuery, you are going to learn how to do it. We are going to write the **Confirm Order** button in an unobtrusive way.

First of all, remove the `data-bind` attribute and add an ID to locate the button:

```html
<button id="confirmOrderBtn" class="btn btn-primary btn-sm">
  Confirm Order
</button>
```

Now write this JavaScript code just over the `applyBindings` method:

```javascript
$(document).on('click', '#confirmOrderBtn').click(function() {
  vm.showOrder();
});
ko.applyBindings(vm);
```

Both the methods are correct; it's the programmer who makes the decision about which paradigm to choose.

If we choose to write our events in a jQuery manner, it is also a good practice to join all your events in files. If you don't have many events, you can have a file called `events.js`, or if you have many events, you can have several files such as `catalog.events.js` or `cart.events.js`.

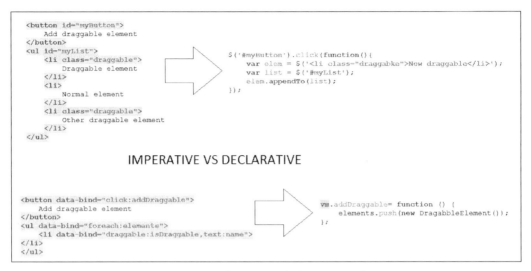

Imperative paradigm versus declarative paradigm

Delegation pattern

When we work with a big amount of data, normal event handling can impact the performance. There is a technique to improve the response time of the events.

When we link the event directly to the item, the browser creates an event for each item. However, we can delegate the event to other elements. Usually, this element can be the document or the parent of the element. In this case, we are going to delegate it to the document that is the event for adding or removing one unit from a product. The problem is that if we just define one event manager for all the products, how do we set the product we are managing? KnockoutJS gives us some useful methods to succeed in this, `ko.dataFor` and `ko.contextFor`.

1. We should update the `cart-item.html` file's add and remove buttons by adding the `add-unit` and `remove-unit` classes respectively:

   ```
   <span class="input-group-addon">
     <div class="btn-group-vertical">
       <button class="btn btn-default btn-xs add-unit">
   ```

```
        <i class="glyphicon glyphicon-chevron-up"></i>
      </button>
      <button class="btn btn-default btn-xs remove-unit">
        <i class="glyphicon glyphicon-chevron-down"></i>
      </button>
    </div>
  </span>
```

2. Then we should add two new events just below the `Confirm Order` event:

    ```
    $(document).on("click", ".add-unit", function() {
      var data = ko.dataFor(this);
      data.addUnit();
    });
    ```

    ```
    $(document).on("click", ".remove-unit", function() {
      var data = ko.dataFor(this);
      data.removeUnit();
    });
    ```

3. Using the `ko.dataFor` method, we can get the same content we obtain with `$data` if we were inside a KnockoutJS context. For more information on unobstrusive event handlers, go to `http://knockoutjs.com/documentation/unobtrusive-event-handling.html`

4. If we want to access the context, we should use `ko.contextFor`; as in this example:

    ```
    $(document).on("click", ".add-unit", function() {
      var ctx = ko.contextFor(this);
      var data = ctx.$data;
      data.addUnit();
    });
    ```

So if we have thousands of products, we continue to have only two event handlers instead of thousands. The following diagram shows how the delegate pattern improves performance..

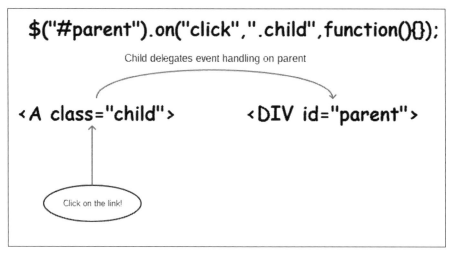

The delegate pattern improves performance

Building custom events

Sometimes we need to make two or more entities of our application communicate with each other, that are not related. For example, we want to keep our cart independent of the application. We can create custom events to update it from the outside and the cart will react to this event; applying the business logic that is required.

We can split the event in two different events: the click and the action. So when we click on the up arrow to add a product, we fire a new custom event that handles the addition of a new unit, and the same to remove it. This give us more information about what is happening in our application, and we realize that a general meaning event such as click just gets the data and sends it to a more specialized event handler that knows what to do with it. This means we can reduce the number of events to just one.

1. Create a `click` event handler at the end of the `viewmodel.js` file that throws a custom event:

```
$(document).on("click", ".add-unit", function() {
  var data = ko.dataFor(this);
  $(document).trigger("addUnit", [data]);
});
```

```
$(document).on("click", ".remove-unit", function() {
  var data = ko.dataFor(this);
  $(document).trigger("removeUnit, [data]);
});

$(document).on("addUnit",function(event, data){
  data.addUnit();
});
$(document).on("removeUnit",function(event, data){
  data.removeUnit();
});
```

Bold lines show how we should use the jQuery trigger method to emit a custom event. Instead of focusing on the element that triggers an action, custom events put the spotlight on the element being acted upon. That gives us some benefits, such as clarity in the code because custom events have a meaning about their behavior in their names (of course we can call an event event1, but we don't like this practice, do we?).

You can read more about custom events and see some examples in the jQuery documentation at http://learn.jquery.com/events/introduction-to-custom-events/.

2. Now that we have defined our events, it is time to move all of them to an isolated file. We call this file cart/events.js. This file will contain all the events of our application.

```
//Event handling
(function() {
  "use strict";
  //Classic event handler
  $(document).on('click','#confirmOrder', function() {
    vm.showOrder();
  });
  //Delegated events
  $(document).on("click", ".add-unit", function() {
    var data = ko.dataFor(this);
    $(document).trigger("addUnit",[data]);
  });
  $(document).on("click", ".remove-unit", function() {
    var data = ko.dataFor(this);
    $(document).trigger("removeUnit, [data]);
  })
  $(document).on("addUnit",function(event, data){
   data.addUnit();
```

```
      });
      $(document).on("removeUnit",function(event, data){
        data.removeUnit();
      });
    })();
```

3. Finally, add the file to the end of the script section just below the `viewmodel.js` script:

```
<script type="text/javascript"
  src="js/cart/events.js"></script>
```

We should notice that now the communication with the cart is done using events, and we have no evidence that there is an object called `cart`. We just know that the object we talk to has an interface that has two methods, `addUnit` and `removeUnit`. We can change the object in the interface (HTML) and if we respect the interface, it will work as we expect.

Events and bindings

We can wrap events and custom events inside `bindingHandlers`. Suppose we want filter products just when we press the *Enter* key. This allows us to reduce the calls we make to the filter method, and if we are making calls to the server, this practice can help us reduce traffic.

Define the custom binding handler in the `custom/koBindings.js` file:

```
ko.bindingHandlers.executeOnEnter = {
  init: function (element, valueAccessor, allBindingsAccessor,
    viewModel) {
    var allBindings = allBindingsAccessor();
    $(element).keypress(function (event) {
      var keyCode = (event.which ? event.which : event.keyCode);
      if (keyCode === 13) {
        allBindings.executeOnEnter.call(viewModel);
        return false;
      }
      return true;
    });
  }
};
```

Since this is an event, we should remember that event initialization can be set in the `init` method itself. We catch the `keypress` event with jQuery and track the key that has been pressed. The key code for the *Enter* key is 13. If we press the *Enter* key, we will call the `executeOnEnter` binding value in the context of the view-model. That is what `allBindings.executeOnEnter.call(viewModel);` does.

Then we need to update our view-model because our filtered catalog is a computed observable that updates itself every time a key goes down. Now we need to convert this computed observable into a simple observable array. So update your `filteredCatalog` variable as follows:

```
//we set a new copy from the initial catalog
var filteredCatalog = ko.observableArray(catalog());
```

Realize the consequence of the following change:

```
var filteredCatalog = catalog();
```

We are not making a copy, but instead we are creating a reference. If we do it that way, we will lose items when we filter the catalog, and we will not be able to get them again.

Now we should create a method that filters the items of the catalog. The code for this function is similar to the computed value we had in the previous version:

```
var filterCatalog = function () {
  if (!catalog()) {
    filteredCatalog([]);
  }
  if (!filter) {
    filteredCatalog(catalog());
  }
  var filter = searchTerm().toLowerCase();
  //filter data
  var filtered = ko.utils.arrayFilter(catalog(), function(item){
    var strProp = ko.unwrap(item["name"]).toLocaleLowerCase();
    if (strProp && (strProp.indexOf(filter) !== -1)) {
      return true;
    }
    return false;
  });
  filteredCatalog(filtered);
};
```

Now add it to the `return` statement:

```
return {
  debug: debug,
  showDebug:showDebug,
  hideDebug:hideDebug,
  searchTerm: searchTerm,
  catalog: filteredCatalog,
  filterCatalog:filterCatalog,
  cart: cart,
  newProduct: newProduct,
  totalItems:totalItems,
  grandTotal:grandTotal,
  addProduct: addProduct,
  addToCart: addToCart,
  removeFromCart:removeFromCart,
  visibleCatalog: visibleCatalog,
  visibleCart: visibleCart,
  showSearchBar: showSearchBar,
  showCartDetails: showCartDetails,
  hideCartDetails: hideCartDetails,
  showOrder: showOrder,
  showCatalog: showCatalog,
  finishOrder: finishOrder
};
```

The last step is to update the search element inside the `catalog.html` template:

```
<div class="input-group" data-bind="visible:showSearchBar">
  <span class="input-group-addon">
    <i class="glyphicon glyphicon-search"></i> Search
  </span>
  <input type="text" class="form-control"
  data-bind="
    textInput: searchTerm,
    executeOnEnter: filterCatalog"
  placeholder="Press enter to search...">
</div>
```

Now, if you write in the search, the input items are not updated; however, when you press *Enter*, the filter is applied.

This is how our folder structure looks after inserting the new code:

Folder structure

Summary

In this chapter, you have learned how to manage events using Knockout and jQuery. You have learned how to combine both technologies to apply different techniques depending on the requirements of your project. We can use declarative paradigms to combine event attaching, `bindingHandlers` and HTML markup, or we can isolate events in the JavaScript code using jQuery events.

In the next chapter, we will address the issue of communicating with the server. You will learn how to validate the input from the user to be sure that we send clean and proper data to the server.

Also we will go through mocking techniques to fake the data server-side. Using mock libraries will help us to develop our frontend application without the necessity for a full operative server. In order to send an AJAX request, we will get a very simple server to run our application because browsers don't allow local AJAX requests by default.

Remember that you can check the code for this chapter at GitHub:

```
https://github.com/jorgeferrando/knockout-cart/tree/chapter4
```

5
Getting Data from the Server

We now have a cart application. To make it work as a real-world app, we need it to get data from a server. However, this book is focused on how to develop a project using KnockoutJS, not on how to configure and run a server.

Fortunately, this situation occurs in every project. Frontend developers begin to work just with the data specification and without any backend servers.

In this chapter, we are going to build a fully-functional frontend communication layer without a server at the backend. To succeed in this task, we are going to mock our data layer with fake objects. When we remove the mock layer, our application will be able to work with real data. This will help us to develop our applications faster and safer: faster because we don't need to wait for a real server response, and safer, because our data manipulation doesn't affect the real server.

REST services

In this chapter, you are going to learn how to make the frontend layer communicate with the backend layer.

You are not building a simple web page. You are building a web application. This means that your project does not only contain data to display to the user, along with some anchors to click on and navigate. This web page also has a logic and model layer behind, and this makes it more complex than a simple web page.

To communicate with the server the frontend uses web services. The **W3C** (short for **World Wide Web Consortium**) defines a web service as a software system designed to support interoperable machine-to-machine interaction over a network. There are many protocols you can use to perform this interaction: SOAP, POX, REST, RPC, and so on.

Nowadays in web development, RESTful services are most used. This is because the **REST** (short for **Representational State Transfer**) protocol has some characteristics that make it easy to use in such apps:

- They are based on URI
- Communication is made using internet media types (usually JSON, but it could be XML or others)
- HTTP methods are standard: `GET`, `POST`, `PUT`, `DELETE`
- It is possible to use hyperlinks to reference the state of a resource

To understand these concepts, we are going to see some examples. Considering the cart scenario, suppose you want to retrieve all your products, do the following:

1. Define the entry point to the API. RESTful protocol is URI based as:

   ```
   http://mydomain.com/api/
   ```

2. Now you want to retrieve all your products, so define a URI that points to this resource as:

   ```
   http://mydomain.com/api/products
   ```

3. Since this is a retrieve operation, the HTTP header should contain the `GET` method as follows:

   ```
   GET /api/products HTTP/1.1
   ```

4. To take advantage of the HTTP protocol, you can send metadata in the header; for example, the type of the data you are sending and the data you want to receive, in the following manner:

   ```
   'Content-Type': 'application/json' //what we send
   Accept: 'application/json; charset=utf-8'//what we expect
   ```

5. The server will respond with some data in the expected format and some information that usually comes within HTTP headers, like the status of the operation: `HTTP/1.1 200 OK`. Following are the formats:
   - 2xx, if all goes fine
   - 4xx, if there is an error on the frontend
   - 5xx, if there is an error on the server side

In case you want to update or delete an object, attach the ID of this object to the URI and use the corresponding header. For example, to edit or delete a product, call this URI using the proper method: `PUT` to edit and `DELETE` to remove. The server will manage these requests properly looking for the information in the URI and headers, for instance:

```
http://mydomain.com/api/products/1
```

To know more about REST and RESTful services, refer to `http://en.wikipedia.org/wiki/Representational_state_transfer`.

Defining CRUD

When you define a service to send and receive data, this object should usually perform a minimum level of behavior. You can identify this behavior through the acronym **CRUD**:

- **Create (C)**: You need to send a message to the server with a new object to persist it in a database. The HTTP POST verb is used for such requests.

- **Retrieve (R)**: The service should be able to send a request to get a collection of objects or just one specific object. The GET verb is used for such requests.

- **Update (U)**: This is a request to update an object. By convention, the PUT verb is used for such requests.

- **Delete (D)**: This is a request to delete an object. The DELETE verb is used for such requests.

More operations can be implemented, and sometimes you do not need to code all CRUD methods. You should adapt your code to the application requirements and define only operations that the application needs. Remember that writing more code than the application needs means creating the possibility of writing more errors in the code.

Singleton resources

In this application, we will refer to resources as objects that are related to the URI contained in the API server. This means that to manage the /products URI we are going to have a ProductResource object that will manage the CRUD operations for this URI.

We will create this object as a singleton to guarantee that we have just one object managing each URI in our application. For more information on singleton, refer to `http://en.wikipedia.org/wiki/Singleton_pattern`.

Setting CRUD operations in the resource

We are going to define some services to define CRUD operations for our products and orders. A common mistake that some developers make is setting CRUD operations within model classes. Best practice says that it is better to separate models and communication layers.

To prepare your project, create a folder called `services`. In this folder, store files that will contain CRUD operations. Perform the following steps:

1. Create two files in the new folder. They represent two communication services: `OrderResource.js` and `ProductResource.js`.

2. Open the `ProductResource.js` file and define basic CRUD operations as follows:

```
var ProductResource = (function () {
  function all() {}
  function get(id) {}
  function create(product) {}
  function update(product) {}
  function remove(id) {}
  return {
    all: all,
    get: get,
    create: create,
    update: update,
    remove: remove
  };
})();
```

This is the skeleton of the CRUD service. You use the `all` and `get` methods to define the retrieve operation. The `all` method will return all the products, and `get` just the product with the ID passed as the parameter. The `create` method will create a product and the `update` method will update a product. The `remove` method will perform the delete operation. We call it `remove` because `delete` is a reserved word in the JavaScript language.

3. To implement the body of these methods, use jQuery AJAX calls (`http://api.jquery.com/jquery.ajax/`). Such requests to the server are asynchronous and use a concept called promise (`http://api.jquery.com/promise/`). A **promise** is just an object that will contain a value in the future. This value is handled by using a callback function.

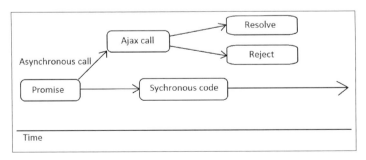

Promise diagram: a promise executes asynchronous code

4. To define the `retrieve` method, you need to define the configuration of the AJAX request. Calling this method will return a promise. You can handle the data contained inside this promise in the view-model in the following manner:

```
function all() {
  return $.ajax({
    dataType:'json',
    type: 'GET',
    url: '/products'
  });
}
function get(id) {
  return $.ajax({
    dataType:'json',
    type: 'GET',
    url: '/products/'+id
  });
}
```

5. Notice that you just need to define the type of response and endpoint that the server has available to get the data (you can see more parameters in the jQuery documentation provided earlier). Also complete the CREATE, UPDATE, and DELETE methods. Remember to respect the verbs (POST, PUT, and DELETE).

```
function create(product) {
  return $.ajax({
    datatype:'json',
    type: 'POST',
    url: '/products',
    data: product
  });
}
function update(product) {
  return $.ajax({
    datatype:'json',
    type: 'PUT',
    url: '/products/'+product.id,
    data: product
  });
}
function remove(id) {
  return $.ajax({
    datatype:'json',
    type: 'DELETE',
    url: '/products/'+id
  });
}
```

Remember that you are building a REST API, so follow the conventions of the architecture. This means that a URL for an entity should be named as a plural.

To get all products, use the `/products` URL. To get just one product, still use the `/products` URL, but also add the ID of the product to the URI. For example, `/products/7` will return the product with the ID number 7. If the relationship is deeper, for example, "the customer 5 has messages", define the route as `/customers/5/messages`. If you want to read the message with ID 1 from user 5, use `/customers/5/message/1`.

There are some cases where you can use singular names, such as `/customers/5/configuration/`, because a user usually has just one configuration. It is up to you to define when words should be pluralized. The only requirement is to be consistent. If you prefer to use all names in the singular you can do so, there is no problem. Pluralizing the name is just a convention, not a rule.

Using resources in the view-model

Now that we have created our product resource, we will use it in our view-model to get our data back by following these steps:

1. First of all, link the `ProductResource.js` file in the `index.html` file, as follows:

   ```
   <script type='text/javascript'
     src='js/resources/ProductResource.js'></script>
   ```

   Since the resource works asynchronously, you can't apply bindings at the end of the file because the data may not be ready yet. Therefore, bindings should be applied when the data has arrived.

   To do this, create a method called `activate`. This method will be fired at the end of the file, on the same line we called `ko.applyBindings` earlier, in the following manner:

   1. Take this line of code:

      ```
      ko.applyBindings(vm);
      ```

   2. Replace it with this one:

      ```
      vm.activate();
      ```

2. Now define the `activate` method in the view-model:

   ```
   var activate = function () {
     ProductResource.all().done(allCallbackSuccess);
   };
   ```

When you call the `all` method a jQuery promise is returned. To manage the results of the promise, jQuery offers a promise API:

- ○ `.done(callback)`: This method is triggered when a promise is resolved with success. This means that a status different from 5xx or 4xx has been received.

- ○ `.fail(callback)`: You can use this method to handle a rejected promise. It is triggered by 5xx and 4xx headers.

- ○ `.then(successCb, errorCb)`: This method gets two callbacks as parameters. The first one is called if the promise is resolved and the second one if the promise is rejected.

- ○ `.always(callback)`: The callback passed to this method runs in both cases.

By using HTTP headers you avoid sending extra information in the body response to know that you have got an error. It is important to know about the protocol you are using (HTTP in this case) and try to use all its advantages, in this case, the possibility of sending information in its header.

3. Now it is time to define the `allCallbackSuccess` method:

```
var allCallbackSuccess = function(response){
  catalog([]);
  response.data.forEach(function(item){
    catalog.push(
      Product (item.id, item.name, item.price, item.stock)
    );
  });
  filteredCatalog(catalog());
  ko.applyBindings(vm);
};
```

A jQuery AJAX callback always has the response as the first parameter. In this case, you get a JSON response with all the items in the catalog.

The first step is to initialize the catalog as an empty array. Once the catalog is initialized, iterate over the collection of items. This collection is stored inside a data object. It is a good practice to isolate data within other variables. This is just in case you want to add metadata to the response. Once you have the catalog ready, link it to the `filteredCatalog` method.

When you we have the initial data ready, that is the moment you can call the `ko.applyBindings` method. If you call it outside the scope of callback you can't be sure that the catalog will have all the items inside. This is because resources perform operations asynchronously and that means that the code is not executed sequentially. It is executed when the promise returned by the resource has data available.

4. The last step is to run the `activate` method at the end of the file, as follows:

```
//ko External Template Settings
infuser.defaults.templateSuffix = '.html';
infuser.defaults.templateUrl = 'views';
vm.activate();
```

If we run our application, it will not work because there is no server to attend to our requests. We will get a 404 error. To solve this problem, we are going to mock our AJAX calls and data.

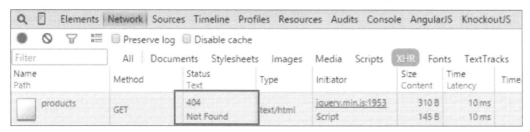

Making AJAX calls without a server behind will throw a 404 error

Using Mockjax to mock HTTP requests

Mocking data just means replacing the `$.ajax` calls with another function that emulates its behavior. Mocking is a commonly-used technique when following a test-driven development paradigm.

To mock jQuery AJAX calls, we are going to use a library called Mockjax. To install Mockjax in the application, follow these steps:

1. Download the library from `https://github.com/jakerella/jquery-mockjax`.

2. Save it into the `vendors` folder.

3. Add a reference in the `index.html` page, just after the jQuery library. To do this, use the `<script>` tag, as shown here:

```
<script type='text/javascript'
  src='vendors/jquery.mockjax.js'></script>
```

4. Create a folder called `mocks` and create a `product.js` file inside it.

5. In the `product.js` file, define a mock calling the `$.mockjax` function, as follows:

```
$.mockjax({
  url: '/products',
  type: 'GET',
  dataType: 'json',
  responseTime: 750,
  responseText: []
});
```

In this definition, you are mocking the request called inside the `ProducResource.all()` method. To define the mock you just need to define these parameters:

  ° **url**: The URL you want to mock

  ° **type**: The type of request

  ° **dataType**: The kind of data you expect

  ° **responseTime**: The duration the response is going to take

  ° **responseText**: The body of the response

Generating mock data with MockJSON

Once you have mocked the HTTP call, you need to send some data in the response. You have different possibilities:

* You can hand-write the data in the `responseText` attribute of the `$.mockjax` call:

```
$.mockjax({
  url: '/products',
  type: 'GET',
  dataType: 'json',
  responseTime: 750,
  responseText: ['Here I can fake the response']
});
```

* You can use a function to generate the mock data:

```
$.mockjax({
  url: '/products',
  type: 'GET',
  dataType: 'json',
  responseTime: 750,
```

```
response: function(settings) {
  var fake = 'We fake the url:'+settings.url;
  this.responseText = fake;
}
});
```

- You can use a library that generates complex and random data in the response.

  This third option can be performed with a library called `mockJSON`. You can download it from the GitHub repository at `https://github.com/mennovanslooten/mockJSON`.

  This library allows you to generate data templates to create random data. This helps you to keep your fake data more realistic. You can see on the screen many different kinds of data. This will help you to check more data display possibilities, such as words that overflow inside containers or text that is too long or too short and appears ugly on the screen.

  - To generate a random element, define a mock template like this:

```
$.mockJSON.generateFromTemplate({
  'data|5-10': [{
    'id|1-100': 0,
    'name': '@PRODUCTNAME',
    'price|10-500': 0,
    'stock|1-9': 0
  }]
});
```

  This template says that you want to generate between 5 and 10 elements that have the following structure:

    - The ID will be a number between 1 and 100

    - The product name will be a value stored in the PRODUCTNAME array

    - The price will be a number between 10 and 500

    - The stock will be a number between 1 and 9

    - To generate the product name array, you just need to add an array or a function to the `$.mockJSON.data` object, as follows:

```
$.mockJSON.data.PRODUCTNAME = [
  'T-SHIRT', 'SHIRT', 'TROUSERS', 'JEANS',
    'SHORTS', 'GLOVES', 'TIE'
];
```

You can generate any kind of data you can imagine. Just create a function and return an array with the values you want to generate, or define a function that generates a random result, a number, a unique ID, and so on.

- ° To return this as a response, attach this template to the response text. Your code should look like this:

```
$.mockJSON.data.PRODUCTNAME = [
  'T-SHIRT', 'SHIRT', 'TROUSERS', 'JEANS', 'SHORTS',
    'GLOVES', 'TIE'
];
$.mockjax({
  url: '/products',
  type: 'GET',
  dataType: 'json',
  responseTime: 750,
  status:200,
  responseText: $.mockJSON.generateFromTemplate({
    'data|5-5': [{
      'id|1-100': 0,
      'name': '@PRODUCTNAME',
      'price|10-500': 0,
      'stock|1-9': 0
    }]
  })
});
```

Add the `mocks/product.js` file at the end of the `index.html` file with the `<script>` tag and see how you get new random data each time you refresh the web page.

When a mock call is done, we see this message in the console

Retrieving a product by ID

To obtain just one product from our API, we are going to fake the `get` method of `ProductResource`. The `ProductResource.get` method will be fired when we click on the name of the product in the catalog list.

This URI has the product's ID in the last segment of the URI. This means that a product with ID=1 will generate a URI like `/products/1`. A product with ID=2 will generate a URI like `/products/2`.

This implies, therefore, that we can't set the URL as a fixed string. We need to use a regular expression.

If you need more information about regular expressions check this link:

`https://developer.mozilla.org/en/docs/Web/JavaScript/Guide/Regular_Expressions`

In order to complete the code to retrieve a product, follow these steps:

1. Add a `mockjax` call to mock the URI. It should use the GET HTTP method. Attach the regular expression to the `url` attribute, as follows:

```
$.mockjax({
  url: /^\/products\/([\d]+)$/,
  type: 'GET',
  dataType: 'json',
  responseTime: 750,
  responseText: ''
});
```

2. Create a template that returns a single product object. To generate a random description you can use the @LOREM_IPSUM magic variable that will return random text. It works in the same way you built the @PRODUCTNAME variable. Let's create a template using the following code:

```
$.mockJSON.generateFromTemplate({
  'data': {
    'id|1-100': 0,
    'name': '@PRODUCTNAME',
    'price|10-500': 0,
    'stock|1-9': 0,
    'description': '@LOREM_IPSUM'
  }
})
```

3. Attach the following template to the `responseText` variable:

```
//URI: /products/:id
$.mockjax({
  url: /^\/products\/([\d]+)$/,
  type: 'GET',
  dataType: 'json',
  responseTime: 750,
  responseText: $.mockJSON.generateFromTemplate({
    'data': {
      'id|1-100': 0,
      'name': '@PRODUCTNAME',
      'price|10-500': 0,
      'stock|1-9': 0,
      'description': '@LOREM_IPSUM'
    }
  })
});
```

4. In the `viewmodel.js` file, create a method that uses the `ProductResource` object to retrieve the product. The method will display an alert box when the data becomes available.

```
var showDescription = function (data) {
  ProductResource.get(data.id())
  .done(function(response){
    alert(response.data.description);
  });
};
```

5. Bind the `showDescription` method to the `catalog.html` template:

```
<td><a href data-bind='click:$parent.showDescription,
  text: name'></a></td>
```

6. Expose the `showDescription` method in the view-model interface:

```
return {
  ...
  showDescription: showDescription,
  ...
};
```

7. Test how you get a description in the alert box.

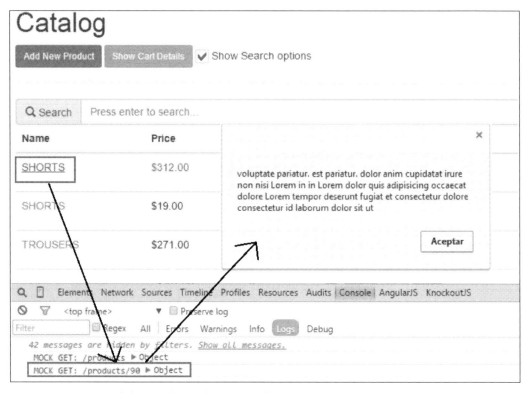

Clicking on the product name will display the product description

Creating a new product

To create a product, follow the same steps as in the previous section:

1. Add an AJAX mock call in the `mocks/product.js` file:

```
$.mockjax({
  url: '/products',
  type:'POST',
  dataType: 'json',
  responseTime: 750,
  status:200,
  responseText: {
    'data': {
      text: 'Product created'
    }
  }
});
```

You should keep in mind some considerations:

- ◦ You should use the POST verb to create an object. Actually, you can use any verb you want, but as per the RESTful API conventions, the POST verb is the one you should use to create new objects.

- ◦ The response text is a message that provides some information about the result.

- ◦ The result itself is managed by the headers:

- ◦ If you get a 2xx value in the status, the done method is fired.

- ◦ If you get a 4xx or 5xx error, the fail method is called.

2. Go to the modelview.js file and update the addProduct function:

```
var addProduct = function (data) {
  var id = new Date().valueOf();
  var product = new Product(
    id,
    data.name(),
    data.price(),
    data.stock()
  );

  ProductResource.create(ko.toJS(data))
  .done(function (response){
    catalog.push(product);
    filteredCatalog(catalog());
    newProduct = Product(new Date().valueOf(),'',0,0);
    $('#addToCatalogModal').modal('hide');
  });
};
```

Obviously, you can't send Knockout observables to the server. To convert objects that contain observables into plain JSON objects, use the ko.toJS function. This function iterates over the objects and extracts the value of each observable.

You can find information about ko.toJS and other methods at http://knockoutjs.com/documentation/json-data.html.

Maybe you have noticed that when you add a new product, the stock goes down by one. This is because when you use the ko.toJS function in the product it executes all functions it has. So, to use it you should avoid methods that manipulate the object and can change its values internally. We are going to solve this issue in the next section.

Test that the application sends data when you call the `addProduct` method.

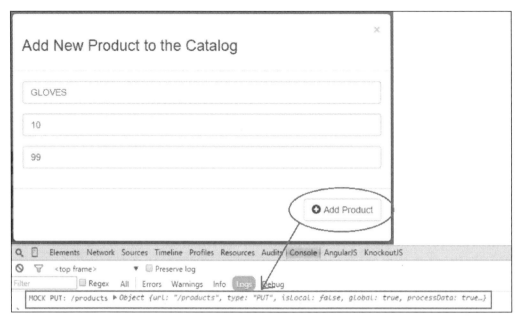

Adding new products uses the AJAX call; pay attention to URL and type fields

Separation of concerns – behavior and data

We have found a problem in our application. When we use the `ko.toJS` function, the result is not as expected. This is a common scenario in software development.

We have made a bad choice setting some logic in our models and we need to fix it. To solve this problem, we are going to separate the data and these behaviors. We are going to use some classes that we will call services.

Services will manage the logic of our models. This means that each model will have a related service that will manage its state.

Creating the product service

If you look in the `models/product.js` file, you can see that the model contains some logic:

```
var hasStock = function () {
  return _product.stock() > 0;
};
var decreaseStock = function () {
  var s = _product.stock();
  if (s > 0) {
    s--;
  }
  _product.stock(s);
};
```

We are going to move this logic and some more to a service with the following steps:

1. Create a folder called `services`.

2. Inside it, create a file called `ProductService`.

3. Create a singleton object and add the `hasStock` and `decreaseStock` functions, as follows:

```
var ProductService = (function() {
  var hasStock = function (product) {
    return product.stock() > 0;
  };

  var decreaseStock = function (product) {
    var s = product.stock();
    if (s > 0) {
      s--;
    }
    product.stock(s);
  };

  return {
    hasStock:hasStock,
    decreaseStock:decreaseStock
  };
})();
```

4. Update the add-to-cart-button component:

```
this.addToCart = function() {
  ...
  if (item) {
    CartProductService.addUnit(item);
  } else {
    item = CartItem(data,1);
    tmpCart.push(item);
    ProductService.decreaseStock(item.product);
  }
  this.cart(tmpCart);
};
```

Notice that you need also to create a service to manage the cart item logic.

Creating the CartProduct service

The cart item service also extracts the logic of the CartProduct model. To create this service, follow these steps:

1. Create a file called CartProductService.js in the service folder.
2. Remove the addUnit and removeUnit methods from the CartProduct model.
3. Update the service with these methods:

```
var CartProductService = (function() {

  var addUnit = function (cartItem) {
    var u = cartItem.units();
    var _stock = cartItem.product.stock();
    if (_stock === 0) {
      return;
    }
    cartItem.units(u+1);
    cartItem.product.stock(--_stock);
  };

  var removeUnit = function (cartItem) {
    var u = cartItem.units();
    var _stock = cartItem.product.stock();
    if (u === 0) {
      return;
    }
    cartItem.units(u-1);
```

```
    cartItem.product.stock(++_stock);
  };

  return {
    addUnit:addUnit,
    removeUnit:removeUnit
  };
})();
```

Updating a product

In our catalog, we will want to update the value of our product. To complete this action, follow these steps:

1. First, to update a product you need to mock the URI that handles the action:

```
$.mockjax({
    url: /^\/products\/([\d]+)$/,
    type:'PUT',
    dataType: 'json',
    responseTime: 750,
    status:200,
    responseText: {
        'data': {
            text: 'Product saved'
        }
    }
});
```

2. Add a button in each row in the `catalog.html` view, in the same cell you have the `add-to-cart-button` component:

```
<button class='btn btn-info' data-bind='click:
  $parent.openEditModal'>
  <i class='glyphicon glyphicon-pencil'></i>
</button>
```

3. Now, open a modal with the data of this product:

```
var openEditModal = function (product) {
  tmpProduct = ProductService.clone(product);
  selectedProduct(product);
  $('#editProductModal').modal('show');
};
```

4. The `tmpProduct` will contain a copy of the object you are going to edit:

```
Var tmpProduct = null;
```

5. The `selectedProduct` will contain the original product you are going to edit:

    ```
    Var selectedProduct = ko.observable();
    ```

6. Create the `clone` function in the `ProductService` resource:

    ```
    var clone = function (product) {
      return Product(product.id(), product.name(),
        product.price(), product.stock());
    };
    ```

7. Create the `refresh` function in the `ProductService` resource. This method allows the service to refresh the product without losing the reference into the cart.

    ```
    var refresh = function (product,newProduct) {
      product.name(newProduct.name());
      product.stock(newProduct.stock());
      product.price(newProduct.price());
    };
    ```

8. Add both methods to the service interface:

    ```
    return {
      hasStock:hasStock,
      decreaseStock:decreaseStock,
      clone:clone,
      refresh: refresh
    };
    ```

9. Create the `edit-product-modal.html` template to display the edit modal. This template is a copy of the `create-product-modal.html` template. You just need to update the form tag line, as follows:

    ```
    <form class='form-horizontal' role='form'
      data-bind='with:selectedProduct'>
    ```

10. You also need to update the `button` bindings:

    ```
    <button type='submit' class='btn btn-default'
      data-bind='click: $parent.cancelEdition'>
      <i class='glyphicon glyphicon-remove-circle'></i> Cancel
    </button>
    <button type='submit' class='btn btn-default'
      data-bind='click: $parent.updateProduct'>
      <i class='glyphicon glyphicon-plus-sign'></i> Save
    </button>
    ```

11. Now, define the `cancelEditon` and the `saveProduct` method:

```
var cancelEdition = function (product) {
  $('#editProductModal').modal('hide');
};
var saveProduct = function (product) {
  ProductResource.save(ko.toJS(product)).done(
    function(response){
    var tmpCatalog = catalog();
    var i = tmpCatalog.length;
    while(i--){
      if(tmpCatalog[i].id() === product.id()){
        ProductService.refresh(tmpCatalog[i],product);
      }
    }
    catalog(tmpCatalog);
    filterCatalog();
    $('#editProductModal').modal('hide');
  });
};
```

12. Finally, add these methods to the view-model API.

Now you can test how to update different values of the product.

Deleting a product

To delete a product, follow some simple steps as you did with the CREATE and UPDATE methods.

1. The first step is to create the mocks in the `mocks/products.js` file, as follows:

```
$.mockjax({
  url: /^\/products\/([\d]+)$/,
  type:'DELETE',
  dataType: 'json',
  responseTime: 750,
  status:200,
  responseText: {
    'data': {
      text: 'Product deleted'
    }
  }
});
```

2. This method is quite easy. Just add a button like the edit button and then the action to remove it.

```
var deleteProduct = function (product){
  ProductResource.remove(product.id())
  .done(function(response){
    catalog.remove(product);
    filteredCatalog(catalog());
    removeFromCartByProduct(product);
  });
};
```

3. Create a function to remove the product from the cart. This function iterates over the cart items and locates the cart item which is related to the removed product. Once this item is located, you can remove it as a normal item using the `removeFromCart` function:

```
var removeFromCartByProduct = function (product) {
  var tmpCart = cart();
  var i = tmpCart.length;
  var item;
  while(i--){
    if (tmpCart[i].product.id() === product.id()){
      item = tmpCart[i];
    }
  }
  removeFromCart(item);
}
```

4. Add a button in the catalog template next to the edit button:

```
<button class='btn btn-danger'
  data-bind='click: $parent.deleteProduct'>
  <i class='glyphicon glyphicon-remove'></i>
</button>
```

Edit and delete buttons

Sending the order to the server

Once you can communicate with the server to manage our products, it's time to send the order. For this purpose, follow these instructions:

1. Create a file named `resources/OrderResource.js` with this content:

```
'use strict';
var OrderResource = (function () {
  function create(order) {
    return $.ajax({
      type: 'PUT',
      url: '/order',
      data: order
    });
  }
  return {
    create: create
  };
})();
```

2. Mock the call by creating a file called `mocks/order.js` and adding this code:

```
$.mockjax({
  type: 'POST',
  url: '/order',
  status: 200,
  responseTime: 750,
  responseText: {
    'data': {
      text: 'Order created'
    }
  }
});
```

3. Update the `finishOrder` method in the `viewmodel.js` file:

```
var finishOrder = function() {
  OrderResource.create().done(function(response){
    cart([]);
    visibleCart(false);
    showCatalog();
    $('#finishOrderModal').modal('show');
  });
};
```

One of the requirements of our application is that the user has the option to update personal data. We are going to allow the user to attach personal data to the order. This is important because when we send an order, we need to know who is going to receive it.

1. Create a new file in the `models` folder called `Customer.js`. It will contain the following function that will generate a customer:

```
var Customer = function () {
  var firstName = ko.observable('');
  var lastName = ko.observable('');
  var fullName = ko.computed(function(){
    return firstName() + ' ' + lastName();
  });
  var address = ko.observable('');
  var email = ko.observable('');
  var zipCode = ko.observable('');
  var country = ko.observable('');
  var fullAddress = ko.computed(function(){
    return address() + ' ' + zipCode() + ', ' + country();
  });
  return {
```

```
        firstName:firstName,
        lastName: lastName,
        fullName: fullName,
        address: address,
        email: email,
        zipCode: zipCode,
        country: country,
        fullAddress: fullAddress,
    };
};
```

2. Link it to the view-model:

```
var customer = Customer();
```

3. Create also an observable array to store the countries that are available to sell:

```
var countries = ko.observableArray(['United States',
    'United Kingdom']);
```

4. Create a form in the order template to show a form to complete the customer data:

```
<div class='col-xs-12 col-sm-6'>
  <form class='form-horizontal' role='form'
    data-bind='with:customer'>
    <div class='modal-header'>
      <h3>Customer Information</h3>
    </div>
    <div class='modal-body'>
      <div class='form-group'>
        <div class='col-sm-12'>
          <input type='text' class='form-control'
            placeholder='First Name'
            data-bind='textInput:firstName'>
        </div>
      </div>
      <div class='form-group'>
        <div class='col-sm-12'>
          <input type='text' class='form-control'
            placeholder='Last Name'
            data-bind='textInput:lastName'>
        </div>
      </div>
      <div class='form-group'>
        <div class='col-sm-12'>
```

```
    <input type='text' class='form-control'
      placeholder='Address'
      data-bind='textInput:address'>
  </div>
</div>
<div class='form-group'>
  <div class='col-sm-12'>
    <input type='text' class='form-control'
      placeholder='Zip code'
      data-bind='textInput:zipCode'>
  </div>
</div>
<div class='form-group'>
  <div class='col-sm-12'>
    <input type='text' class='form-control'
      placeholder='Email'
      data-bind='textInput:email'>
  </div>
</div>
<div class='form-group'>
  <div class='col-sm-12'>
    <select class='form-control' data-bind='options:
      $parent.countries,value:country'></select>
  </div>
</div>
    </div>
  </form>
</div>
```

5. Send this information with the order request using the `finishOrder` method:

```
var finishOrder = function() {
  var order = {
    cart: ko.toJS(cart),
    customer: ko.toJS(customer)
  };
  OrderResource.create(order).done(function(response){
    cart([]);
    hideCartDetails();
    showCatalog();
    $('#finishOrderModal').modal('show');
  });
};
```

Our AJAX communication is complete. Now you can add and remove the `mocks/*.` `js` files from your project to get fake data or real data. While using this method, you don't need to have a server running behind your application when you are developing frontend issues.

Once personal data is provided you can close the order

Handling AJAX errors

We have built the happy path of our application. But in the real world an error can occur during communication with the server. To manage this there are two ways:

- The `fail` method of the AJAX promise:

```
ProductResource.remove()
.done(function(){...})
.fail(function(response){
  console.error(response);
  alert("Error in the communication. Check the console!");
});
```

- A global AJAX error handler:

```
$(document).ajaxError(function(event,response) {
  console.error(response);
  alert("Error in the communication. Check the console!");
});
```

If you have a consistent error format, the global handler is a very good choice to handle errors.

To test an error, update the status attribute of one mock from 200 to 404 or 501:

```
$.mockjax({
  url: /^\/products\/([\d]+)$/,
  type:"DELETE",
  dataType: "json",
  responseTime: 750,
  status:404,
  responseText: {
    "data": {
      text: "Product deleted"
    }
  }
});
```

Validating data

Now you can send and receive data, but what happens if the user sets some data that is not allowed on the server? You have no control over user input. It is important that if some values are not allowed, you alert the user to it. To validate Knockout data, there is a library called Knockout Validation (which can be found at `https://github.com/Knockout-Contrib/Knockout-Validation`) that makes this very easy.

This library extends the observables with some values that allow you to validate the data when it changes. We are now going to update our models to add some kind of validation.

Extending the product model

To validate our models using the Knockout Validation library, we are going to extend our model's attributes. **Extenders** are a basic feature of Knockout. Using extenders we can add some properties to our observables to increase their behavior. For more information on extenders, please refer to the following link:

`http://knockoutjs.com/documentation/extenders.html`

We are going to extend our product model with some properties that will allow us to validate data by following these steps:

1. Go to the `models/Product.js` file.

2. Update the `name` field. It should have at least three letters and should contain just letters, numbers, and dashes:

    ```
    _name = ko.observable(name).extend({
    ```

```
    required: true,
    minLength: 3,
    pattern: {
      message: 'Hey this doesn\'t match my pattern',
      params: '^[A-Za-z0-9 \-]+$'
    }
})
```

3. Update the `price` to allow just numbers, and set a range (maximum and minimum values) for it:

```
_price = ko.observable(price).extend({
    required: true,
    number:true,
    min: 1
}),
```

4. Do the same with the `stock`:

```
_stock = ko.observable(stock).extend({
    required: true,
    min: 0,
    max: 99,
    number: true
})
```

5. Create a validation group to know when the full object is valid:

```
var errors = ko.validation.group([_name, _price, _stock]);
```

This error variable will contain an observable array. When this array has no elements, all observables have a correct value.

6. In the `add-to-catalog-modal.html` template, enable the create button only if all values in the product are valid:

```
<button type='submit' class='btn btn-default'
  data-bind='click:$parent.addProduct,
  enable:!errors().length'>
  <i class='glyphicon glyphicon-plus-sign'></i> Add Product
</button>
```

7. Add the same button to the `edit-product-modal.html` template:

```
<button type='submit' class='btn btn-default'
  data-bind='enable:!errors().length, click:
  $parent.saveProduct'>
  <i class='glyphicon glyphicon-plus-sign'></i> Save
</button>
```

8. If you want to set a style for the error messages, you just need to define CSS rules for the `validationMessage` class, as follows. A `span` element will be shown next to the element that is bound with the validated observable:

```
.validationMessage { color: Red; }
```

Extending the customer model

You also need to validate the customer data. These are the rules for validation:

- A first name is required
- A last name is required and it needs a minimum of three characters
- An a ddress is required and it needs a minimum of five characters
- An e-mail address is required and must match the built-in e-mail pattern
- The zip code is required and must contain five numbers

To achieve this task, make some updates in the code, as follows:

1. Extend the customer object in the `models/Customer.js` file:

```
var firstName = ko.observable('').extend({
  required: true
});
var lastName = ko.observable('').extend({
  required: true,
  minLength: 3
});
var fullName = ko.computed(function(){
  return firstName() + ' ' + lastName();
});
var address = ko.observable('').extend({
  required: true,
  minLength: 5
});
var email = ko.observable('').extend({
  required: true,
  email: true
});
var zipCode = ko.observable('').extend({
  required: true,
  pattern: {
    message: 'Zip code should have 5 numbers',
    params: '^[0-9]{5}$'
  }
});
```

```
var country = ko.observable('');
var fullAddress = ko.computed(function(){
    return address() + ' ' + zipCode() + ', ' + country();
});
var errors = ko.validation.group([firstName, lastName,
  address, email, zipCode]);
```

2. Enable the buy button if the customer data is completed and valid in the `order.html` template:

```
<button class='btn btn-sm btn-primary'
  data-bind='click:finishOrder,
  enable:!customer.errors().length'>
  Buy & finish
</button>
```

3. Show the user information in the `finish-order-modal.html` template:

```
<div class='modal-body'>
  <h2>Your order has been completed!</h2>
  <p>It will be sent to:</p>
  <p>
    <b>Name: </b><span data-bind='text:
      customer.fullName'></span><br/>
    <b>Address: </b><span data-bind='text:
      customer.fullAddress'></span><br/>
    <b>Email: </b><span data-bind='text:
      customer.email'></span><br/>
  </p>
</div>
```

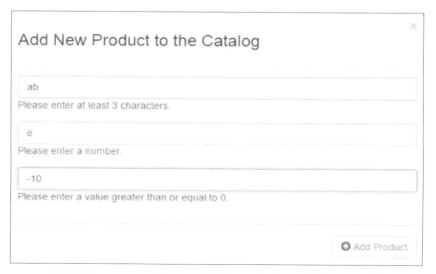

Validation messages that appear if information in the fields is not valid

Now our models are validated and we know that the data we are sending has a valid format.

To view the complete code of the application, you can download the code of this chapter from `https://github.com/jorgeferrando/knockout-cart/tree/chapter5`.

Summary

In this chapter, you learned how to communicate with our application using jQuery to perform AJAX calls. You also learned how easy it is to apply validation to our models using the Knockout Validation library, which uses the `extend` method native to Knockout to increase the behavior of observables.

You experienced one of the problems that KnockoutJS has: you need to serialize the objects to send them to the server and you need to wrap them in observables when they come from the server. To solve this, you have the `ko.toJS` method, but this implies having objects without code that allows them to update their values.

In the next chapter, you will learn how to manage dependencies between files using RequireJS and the module pattern.

6
The Module Pattern – RequireJS

We can say now that our application has all the functionality we mentioned in the *Chapter 1, Refreshing the UI Automatically with KnockoutJS*. What we have done in the last four chapters is a very good approach to solving code design in small projects. The code is tidy and the folder structure is also cohesive. The code is easy to read and follow.

However, when projects begin to grow this approach is not enough. You need to keep the code tidy, not just in the file and folder structure, but logically as well.

In this chapter, we are going to modularize our code to keep the different parts of our application isolated and reusable. We will also see how to keep our context cleaner.

Now the project begins to look more complex. It is important to know the tools that help you to debug the code when you find an error. In the first part of the chapter, you will learn about tools that can help you to inspect your KnockoutJS code. You will use a browser plugin (Chrome Extension) to analyze the code.

In the second part of the chapter, you will convert your files into modules. That will help you to keep each part of the application isolated from the others. You will use a pattern called 'dependency injection' to solve dependencies between modules. Learn more about this pattern at `http://en.wikipedia.org/wiki/Dependency_injection`.

In the last part, you will learn how to create modules following the Asynchronous Module Definition (AMD) specification. To create modules following the AMD specification, you will use a library called RequireJS. This library will manage all dependencies between the different modules. For more about AMD, refer to `http://en.wikipedia.org/wiki/Asynchronous_module_definition`.

Installing the Knockout context debugger extension

In the previous chapters, you created a simple debugger to show the state of your view-model. This is very useful to see the state of our application quickly. With the debug binding, you don't need to open the extension tools to check what is happening to your data. But you often isolate just a part of the application or see what is happening with the models bound to a DOM element.

In Google Chrome, you have a very good extension called **KnockoutJS context debugger**, which can be downloaded from `https://chrome.google.com/webstore/detail/knockoutjs-context-debugg/oddcpmchholgcjgjdnfjmildmlielhof`.

This extension allows you to view the bindings of each DOM node and trace online the changes in your view-model through the console. Install it and restart the Chrome browser.

Check in chrome://extensions whether KnockoutJS context debugger has been installed

To check the context bound to your models, open **Chrome Developer Tools** by pressing *F12* and opening the **Elements** tab. You will see two panels. The left one has the DOM schema. The right panel has different tabs. By default, the **Styles** tab opens. Select the tab that says **Knockout context**. There, you should see all the bindings added to the root context.

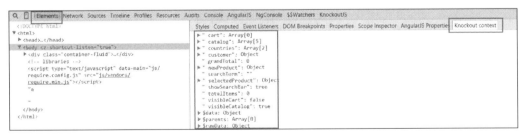

How to show a KnockoutJS context that is bound to a DOM element

If you select a `<tr>` element from your catalog, you will navigate deeper into the context and be inside the catalog item scope. You will not be able to see the `$root` context; you will see the `$data` context. You can navigate up through the `$parent` element or change the element in the DOM panel.

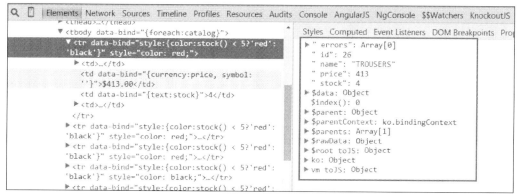

You can easily inspect item context inside foreach bindings

You can also see the `ko` object. This is a good way to navigate through the Knockout API.

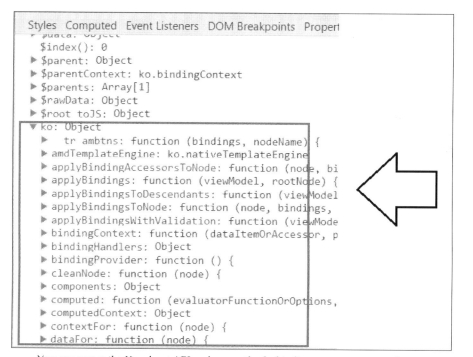

You can access the Knockout API and see methods, bindings, components, and so on

Now locate the **KnockoutJS** tab (it is in the same collection as the **Elements** tab). Press the **Enable Tracing** button. This function allows you to follow real-time changes in the view-model. Changes are painted in the console.

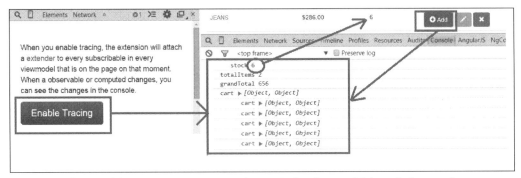

If you enable tracing, you can capture changes in the view-model through the console

Also, you can measure time and performance using the **Timeline** tab. You can see how much time the application uses to render DOM elements when a change is made in the model.

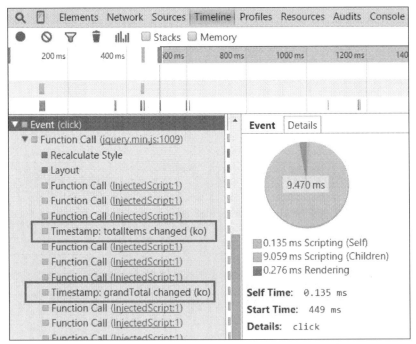

With tracing enabled, you can record events and obtain useful information

Now that you have learned about this plugin, we can delete (or keep, it's your choice) the debug binding we built before.

The console

The **console** is one of the most important tools for developers. You can use it to check the state of our application while it is in use.

You can locate the JavaScript code and set breakpoints to check what is happening at a particular point. You can do this by locating the JavaScript file in the **Sources** tab. Just click the line you want to stop at. Then you can check the value of the variables and run the code step by step. Also, you can write the word `debugger` in the code to stop the program at this place.

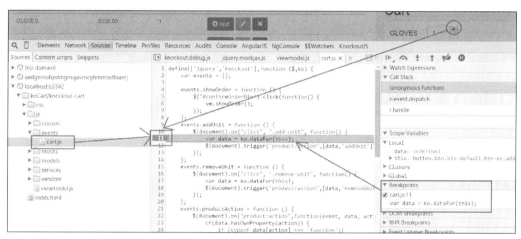

You can set breakpoints in the code and check the values of variables

If you navigate to the **Console** tab you will see the console itself. There, you can show information using the `console.log` function or check the console object documentation to see the best method you can use at each moment (`https://developer.mozilla.org/en-US/docs/Web/API/Console`).

If you write the word `window` in the console, you will see all the objects that are in the global scope.

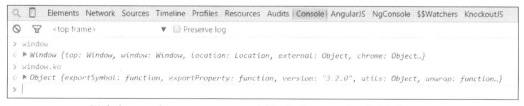

With the console, you can access variables in the current and global context

You can write the word vm (the view-model) to see the vm object we have created.

```
> vm
  ▶ Object {debug: function, showDebug: function, hideDebug: function, searchTerm: function, catalog: function…}
> Product()
  ▶ Object {id: function, name: function, price: function, stock: function, hasStock: function…}
> ProductService()
  ▶ Object {all: function, get: function, create: function, save: function, remove: function}
> customerData
  ▶ Object {firstName: function, lastName: function, fullName: function, address: function, email: function…}
```

All components are set in the global scope

But you can also write `Product` or `ProductService` or anything we have created and you will see it. When you have a lot of information, to have all your objects at the top level can be chaotic. Defining namespaces and keeping a hierarchy is a good practice to keep your components isolated. You should keep just an entry point to the application.

The module pattern

This pattern allows us to focus on which part of the code is exposed out of the class (public elements) and which parts of the code are hidden to the final user (private elements).

This pattern is commonly used in JavaScript software development. It is applied in popular libraries like jQuery, Dojo, and ExtJS.

This pattern has a very clear structure and is very easy to apply once you know how to use it. Let's apply the module pattern in our application:

1. First, define the name of your module. If you define the module in different files, it is important to define and initialize it applying a pattern that allows it to be extensible. Using the || operator in the initialization indicates that the ModuleName value will be assigned to itself if it has a value. If it hasn't got a value it means that this is the first time it has been created, so assign to it a default value—in this case an empty object:

```
var ModuleName;
ModuleName = ModuleName || {};
```

2. Then, define each component of the module. It can be a function, a variable, or another module:

```
ModuleName.CustomComponent = function () {
};
ModuleName.CustomProperty = 10;
ModeleName.ChildModule = OtherModule;
```

3. Finally, insert the dependencies of the module using the dependency injection pattern. This pattern passes all module dependencies as parameters and invokes the function immediately:

```
ModuleName.CustomComponent = (function (dependency){
  //Component code
})(dependency);
```

4. This how a complete module looks:

```
var ModuleName;
var ModuleName = ModuleName || {};
ModuleName.CustomComponent = (function(dependency){
  //Component code
})(dependency);
```

5. To define a component, return the component object. The first pattern to define your component is to use the revealing module pattern. It consists of returning an object to the end of the function that contains only the public interface. These are singleton objects:

```
ModuleName.CustomComponent = (function(dependency){
  var somePrivateProperty = 1;
  var method1 = function(){
    dependency.methodFromDependency();
  };
  return {
    method1:method1,
    method2:method2
  }
})(dependency);

You can also define objects that can be instantiated using the new
operator:  ModuleName.CustomComponent = (function(dependency){
  var component = function (a,b,c) {
    var somePrivateProperty=1;
    this.someMethod = function(){
      dependency.methodFromDependency()
    }
    this.otherMethod(){
      return a+b*c;
    }
    return this;
  }

  return component;
})(dependency);
//We can instantiate the component as an object
//var instance = new ModuleName.CustomComponent(x,y,z);
```

Creating the Shop module

To modularize our application, we are going to create a module called Shop that will contain our entire application. This module will contain other submodules and components. This hierarchical structure will help you to keep coherence in your code.

As the first approach, group your components by file and by type. This means that each component of the modules will be in a file and the files will be grouped by type in a folder. For example, there is a folder named services. This means that all services will be in this folder, and each service will be completely defined in one file. As a convention, the components will have the same name as the file in which they are, without the extension of course.

Actually, the files are already grouped by type so this is a job you don't need to do again. We are going to focus our efforts on converting our files into modules.

The ViewModel module

We have just one view-model in our application. This is a component where we can apply the singleton module approach.

We are going to carefully create our first module step by step:

1. Open the `viewmodel.js` file.

2. Define the Shop module, which is the top module of our application:

   ```
   var Shop;
   ```

3. Initialize the Shop module by applying the extension pattern:

   ```
   Shop = Shop || {};
   ```

4. Define the ViewModel component:

   ```
   Shop.ViewModel = (function(){})();
   ```

5. Set the code from the unmodularized view-model version inside the module:

   ```
   Shop.ViewModel = (function(){
     var debug = ko.observable(false);
     var showDebug = function () {
       debug(true);
     };

     var hideDebug = function () {
       debug(false);
     };
   ```

```
        var visibleCatalog = ko.observable(true);
        // ... the rest of the code
        return {
          debug: debug,
          showDebug:showDebug,
          hideDebug:hideDebug,
          searchTerm: searchTerm,
          catalog: filteredCatalog,
    ....
        };
    })();
```

6. You have not converted other files into modules, but you are now going to add dependencies into the module:

```
Shop.ViewModel = (function (ko, Models, Services,
    Resources){
    //code of the module
}) (ko, Shop.Models, Shop.Services, Shop.Resources);
```

7. At the end of the file, outside the module, initialize the template, validation, and objects:

```
$(document).ajaxError(function(event,response) {
    console.error(response);
    alert("Error in the communication. Check the console!");
});

//ko External Template Settings
infuser.defaults.templateSuffix = ".html";
infuser.defaults.templateUrl = "views";

ko.validation.init({
    registerExtenders: true,
    messagesOnModified: true,
    insertMessages: true,
    parseInputAttributes: true
});
var vm = Shop.ViewModel;
vm.activate();
```

You need to update two methods in our view-model: the `activate` method and the `allCallbackSuccess` method. The reason you need to update these methods is because in the `allCallbackSuccess` method you need to run the `ko.applyBindings` method, and `allCallbackSuccess` has no access to the this object because it is out of the scope.

To solve this, we are going to use the same technique we used with the click binding to attach more parameters. We are going to use the `bind` JavaScript method to bind the `allCallbackSuccess` method to the this object. Therefore, we will be able to run the `ko.applyBindings` using the this object as done in the following code:

```
var allCallbackSuccess = function(response){
  catalog([]);
  response.data.forEach(function(item){
    catalog.push(Product(
      item.id,item.name,item.price,item.stock));
  });
  filteredCatalog(catalog());
  if (catalog().length) {
    selectedProduct(catalog()[0]);
  }
  ko.applyBindings(this);
};

var activate = function () {
  ProductResource.all()
  .done(allCallbackSuccess.bind(this));
};
```

Using this pattern you can convert any piece of code into an isolated and portable module. The next step is to create the `Models` module, the `Services` module, and the `Resources` module.

The Models module

As we have done with the view-model, we are going to convert each model into a component and we are going to wrap it inside a module called `Models`, the following steps:

1. Open the `models/product.js` file.

2. Define our top-level module, `Shop`, and initialize it:
   ```
   var Shop;
   Shop = Shop || {};
   ```

3. Then create the `Models` namespace. It will be an object or the value it has before, in case it exists:
   ```
   Shop.Models = Shop.Models || {};
   ```

4. Define the product model with its dependencies. Remember, the first value is the product itself. This allows us to extend the model in case we use many files to define it. So, we define the product model as follows:

```
Shop.Models.Product = (function(){

})()
```

5. Pass the dependencies. This time you just need to use the Knockout dependency to use observables. Knockout is a global object and there is no need to add it to the dependencies, but it is a good practice to do it as in the following code:

```
Shop.Models.Product = (function (ko){
}(ko)
```

6. Finally, set the code we had in the `models/Product.js` file earlier:

```
var Shop;
Shop = Shop || {};
Shop.Models = Shop.Models || {};
Shop.Models.Product = (function (ko){
  return function (id, name, price, stock) {
    _id = ko.observable(id).extend(...);
    _name = ko.observable(name).extend(...);
    _price = ko.observable(price).extend(...);
    _stock = ko.observable(error).extend(...);
    var errors = ko.validation.group([_name, _price, _stock]);
    return {
      id: _id,
      name: _name,
      price: _price,
      stock: _stock,
      errors: errors
    };
  };
}) (ko);
```

Follow the same steps to convert the `models/CartProduct.js` and `models/Customer.js` files into modules. Models are perfect candidates to apply the pattern we use to generate instantiable objects.

It is important that you keep the consistency between components and file names. Be sure that your files have the name of the component they contain with the `.js` extension.

Here is the final result of converting the `models/CartProduct.js` file:

```javascript
var Shop;
Shop = Shop || {};
Shop.Models = Shop.Models || {};
Shop.Models.CartProduct = (function(ko){

  return function (product,units){
    var
    _product = product,
    _units = ko.observable(units)
    ;

    var subtotal = ko.computed(function(){
      return _product.price() * _units();
    });

    return {
      product: _product,
      units: _units,
      subtotal: subtotal
    };
  }
})(ko);
```

Also take a look at the result of the `models/Customer.js` file:

```javascript
var Shop;
Shop = Shop || {};
Shop.Models = Shop.Models || {};
Shop.Models.Customer = (function(ko){
  return function() {
    var firstName = ko.observable("John").extend({
      required: true
    });
    var lastName = ko.observable("Doe").extend({
      required: true,
      minLength: 3
    });
    var fullName = ko.computed(function(){
      return firstName() + " " + lastName();
    });
    var address = ko.observable("Baker Street").extend({
      required: true,
      minLength: 5
```

```
    });
    var email = ko.observable("john@doe.com").extend({
      required: true,
      email: true
    });
    var zipCode = ko.observable("12345").extend({
      required: true,
      minLength: 3,
      pattern: {
        message: 'Zip code should have 5 numbers',
        params: '^[0-9]{5}$'
      }
    });
    var country = ko.observable("");
    var fullAddress = ko.computed(function(){
      return address() + " " + zipCode() + ", " + country();
    });
    var errors = ko.validation.group([firstName,
      lastName, address, email, zipCode]);
    return {
      firstName:firstName,
      lastName: lastName,
      fullName: fullName,
      address: address,
      email: email,
      zipCode: zipCode,
      country: country,        fullAddress: fullAddress,
      errors: errors
    };
  };
})(ko);
```

The Resources module

In terms of code, building a module that contains a model and building one that contains a resource is not so different. The module pattern applied is the same. Nevertheless, you don't need to create instances of the resources. To apply CRUD operations to the models, you just need an object that handles this responsibility. Therefore, the resources will be singletons, as done in the following steps:

1. Open the `resources/ProductResource.js` file.

2. Create the top hierarchy module:

```
var Shop;
Shop = Shop || {};
```

3. Create the `Resources` namespace:

```
Shop.Resources = Shop.Resources || {};
```

4. Define `ProductResource` using the module pattern:

```
Shop.Resources.ProductResource = (function(){
})()
```

5. Set the dependencies. In this case, jQuery is the dependency you need. jQuery is a global object and you don't need to pass it as a dependency, but it's a good practice to do so.

```
Shop.Resources.ProductResource = (function($){
}(jQuery);
```

6. Finally, set the following code in the `resources/ProductResource.js` file. Since in our application resources are singleton, extend the resource with the methods used in the following code:

```
var Shop;
Shop = Shop || {};
Shop.Resources = Shop.Resources || {};
Shop.Resources.ProductResource = (function($){

  function all() {
    return $.ajax({
      type: 'GET',
      url: '/products'
    });
  }
  function get(id) {
    return $.ajax({
      type: 'GET',
      url: '/products/'+id
    });
  }
  function create(product) {
    return $.ajax({
      type: 'POST',
      url: '/products',
      data: product
    });
  }
```

```
    function save(product) {
      return $.ajax({
        type: 'PUT',
        url: '/products/'+product.id,
        data: product
      });
    }
    function remove(id) {
      return $.ajax({
        type: 'DELETE',
        url: '/products/'+id
      });
    }
    return {
      all:all,
      get: get,
      create: create,
      save: save,
      remove: remove
    };
  }(jQuery);
```

Now apply the same steps to the `OrderResouce` component. You can see the final result in this piece of code:

```
var Shop;
Shop = Shop || {};
Shop.Resources = Shop.Resources || {};
Shop.Resources.OrderResource = (function ($) {
  function save(order) {
    return $.ajax({
      type: 'PUT',
      url: '/order',
      data: order
    });
  }
  return {
    save: save
  };
}) (jQuery);
```

The Services module

Services are also singletons, like resources, so follow the same steps as the resources module:

1. Open the `services/ProductService.js` file.

2. Create the top hierarchy module:

```
var Shop;
Shop = Shop || {};
```

3. Create the `Resources` namespace:

```
Shop.Services = Shop.Services || {};
```

4. Define `ProductService`:

```
Shop.Services.ProductService = (function(){
}) ();
```

5. In this case the service has no dependencies.

6. Finally, set the following code in the `services/ProductService.js` file. Since in the application the resources are singleton, extend the resource with the methods used in the following code:

```
var Shop;
Shop = Shop || {};
Shop.Services = Shop.Services || {};
Shop.Services.ProductService = (function(Product) {
  var hasStock = function (product) {
    return product.stock() > 0;
  };

  var decreaseStock = function (product) {
    var s = product.stock();
    if (s > 0) {
      s--;
    }
    product.stock(s);
  };

  var clone = function (product) {
    return Product(product.id(), product.name(),
      product.price(), product.stock());
  };

  var refresh = function (product, newProduct) {
```

```
      product.name(newProduct.name());
      product.stock(newProduct.stock());
      product.price(newProduct.price());
    };

    return {
      hasStock:hasStock,
      decreaseStock:decreaseStock,
      clone:clone,
      refresh: refresh
    };
  })(Shop.Models.Product);
```

Events, bindings, and Knockout components

We are not going to modularize events, because they are specific to this application. It makes no sense to isolate something that is not portable. We will not modularize either bindings or components because they are injected into the Knockout object as part of the library, so they are isolated enough and they aren't part of the modules, but the Knockout object. But we need to update dependencies in all these files because different parts of the application are now isolated in the Shop module and its submodules.

Updating the add-to-cart-button component

To update the component with new namespaces, update (overwrite) the references to the dependencies, as follows:

```
ko.components.register('add-to-cart-button', {
  viewModel: function(params) {
    this.item = params.item;
    this.cart = params.cart;
    this.addToCart = function() {
      var CartProduct = Shop.Models.CartProduct;
      var CartProductService = Shop.Services.CartProductService;
      var ProductService = Shop.Services.ProductService;

      var data = this.item;
```

```
      var tmpCart = this.cart();
      var n = tmpCart.length;
      var item = null;

      if(data.stock()<1) {
        return;
      }
      while(n--) {
        if (tmpCart[n].product.id() === data.id()) {
          item = tmpCart[n];
        }
      }
      if (item) {
        CartProductService.addUnit(item);
      } else {
        item = CartProduct(data,1);
        tmpCart.push(item);
        ProductService.decreaseStock(item.product);
      }
      this.cart(tmpCart);
    };
  },
  template:
    '<button class="btn btn-primary"
      data-bind="click:addToCart">
      <i class="glyphicon glyphicon-plus-sign"></i> Add
    </button>'
});
```

Updating events

Update those lines of code that have dependencies from the new modules, as follows:

```
(function() {
  "use strict";
  $(document).on("click","#confirmOrderBtn", function() {
    vm.showOrder();
  });
  $(document).on("click", ".add-unit", function() {
    var data = ko.dataFor(this);
    $(document).trigger("addUnit",[data]);
  });
  $(document).on("click", ".remove-unit", function() {
```

```
        var data = ko.dataFor(this);
        $(document).trigger("removeUnit",[data]);
    });
    $(document).on("addUnit",function(event, data){
        Shop.Services.CartProductService.addUnit(data);
    });
    $(document).on("removeUnit",function(event, data){
        Shop.Services.CartProductService.removeUnit(data);
    });
})();
```

You have learned a very good pattern to manage dependencies without any external tools. You can use it in almost all your projects. It will work better if you combine all your files into one.

This book is not going to cover how to join and minify files to use them in a production environment. Joining and minifying files improves the performance of applications because minifying reduces the size of files and joining them reduces the number of HTTP calls to one.

To do this you can use Node.js (`http://nodejs.org/`) and a build module like Grunt (`http://gruntjs.com/`) or Gulp (`http://gulpjs.com/`). If you are interested in learning about deployment practices like minification, combination of files, and so on, there is a large bibliography about Node.js and deployment tools on the Internet.

To access the code of this part of the chapter, go to the GitHub repository at

`https://github.com/jorgeferrando/knockout-cart/tree/chapter6Part1`.

Using RequireJS to manage dependencies

In the previous section, you learned how to isolate different parts of the code. You also grouped the files by type and component names, which follow a consistent pattern. However, you have not solved one important problem that grows in proportion to the size of the project. To give you a clue about what this problem is, let's see our `index.html` file. Look at the part of the `<script>` tags section:

```
<script type="text/javascript" src="js/vendors/jquery.min.js"></
script>
<script type="text/javascript" src="js/vendors/jquery.mockjax.js"></
script>
<script type="text/javascript" src="js/vendors/jquery.mockjson.js"></
script>
<script type="text/javascript" src="js/vendors/icheck.js"></script>
<script type="text/javascript" src="js/vendors/bootstrap.min.js"></
```

```
    script>
    <script type="text/javascript" src="js/vendors/knockout.debug.js"></
    script>
    ...
    ...
    ...
    <script type="text/javascript" src="js/resources/ProductResource.
    js"></script>
    <script type="text/javascript" src="js/resources/OrderResource.js"></
    script>
    <script type="text/javascript" src="js/viewmodel.js"></script>
    <script type="text/javascript" src="js/events/cart.js"></script>
```

You need to keep dependencies between all these files manually. The complexity of doing this grows as the project does. Therefore, there is a problem when you need to know the dependencies of all your files. This can be handled easily in small projects, but when working on big projects this can be a nightmare. Also, if you load all your files at the beginning, starting your application can be penalized.

To solve this problem, there are multiple libraries that can help. We are going to use RequireJS (refer to `http://requirejs.org/` for more information), which is focused on loading scripts asynchronously and managing dependencies. It follows AMD to write different modules. This means it uses the `define` and `require` statements to define and load different modules. AMD libraries are focused on the client side of applications and help load JavaScript modules when needed. For more information on AMD, please visit the following link:

`http://en.wikipedia.org/wiki/Asynchronous_module_definition`

This is very helpful because it optimizes the number of requests made. This enables the application to start faster and load just the modules that the user needs.

There is another pattern to define asynchronous modules, called CommonJS (learn more about it at `http://requirejs.org/docs/commonjs.html`), which is used by default by Node.js modules. You can use this definition in the client-side application using Node.js and a library called **browserify** (learn more about it at `http://browserify.org/`).

In this book, we are going to focus on RequireJS, because it doesn't require Node.js or any compilation and is commonly used in client-side applications.

Updating the template engine

Unfortunately, the `ExternalTemplateEngine` we have used until now is not AMD compatible. This is why you should use other solutions. There is a KnockoutJS extension called amd-helpers. You can download it from `https://github.com/rniemeyer/knockout-amd-helpers`. Ryan Niemeyer is the author of this extension. He is a very famous Knockout developer and has a large following in the Knockout community. He has a blog called Knockmeout (`http://knockmeout.net`) which has a large number of articles about Knockout and good examples of how the amd-helpers library should be used. In this book, we are just going to use the template engine. But this extension has many other features.

RequireJS just loads JavaScript files natively. To load HTML files asynchronously, download the text extension from `https://github.com/requirejs/text` and add it to the `vendors` folder. With this extension, you can load any kind of file as text.

Now, when we need to load a text file we just need to add the prefix `text!` before the path of the file.

Configuring RequireJS

To configure RequireJS, create a file at the same level as the `viewmodel.js` file lies. You can call it `main.js`, and follow these steps:

1. Define the basic `config` method:

   ```
   require.config({

   });
   ```

2. Then, define the base URL for the scripts. This is where RequireJS will look for scripts:

   ```
   Require.config({
   baseUrl:'js'
   });
   ```

3. Now, define aliases for the paths of the vendor libraries in the `paths` attribute. This helps you to avoid writing long paths in our module dependencies. You don't need to define the extension. RequireJS adds the extension for you:

   ```
   require.config({
     baseUrl:'js',
     paths: {
       bootstrap:'vendors/bootstrap.min',
       icheck: 'vendors/icheck',
   ```

```
         jquery: 'vendors/jquery.min',
         mockjax: 'vendors/jquery.mockjax',
         mockjson: 'vendors/jquery.mockjson',
         knockout  : 'vendors/knockout.debug',
         'ko.validation':'vendors/ko.validation',
         'ko-amd-helpers': 'vendors/knockout-amd-helpers',
         text: 'vendors/require.text'
      }
   });
```

4. Also, define dependencies inside the `shim` property. This tells RequireJS which files must be loaded before a library is loaded:

```
require.config({
   baseUrl:'js',
   paths: {
      ...
   },
   shim: {
      'jquery': {
         exports: '$'
      },
      bootstrap: {
         deps:['jquery']
      },
      mockjax: {
         deps:['jquery']
      },
      mockjson: {
         deps:['jquery']
      },
      knockout: {
         exports: 'ko',
         deps:['jquery']
      },
      'ko.validation':{
         deps:['knockout']
      },
      'ko.templateEngine': {
```

```
        deps:['knockout']
      }
    },
  });
```

5. Define the file that should be called when the configuration is done. In this case the file is `app.js`. This file will be the entry point of the application and will trigger all the dependencies that load at the start of our project:

```
//write this inside main.js file
require.config({
  baseUrl:'js',
  paths: {...},
  shim: {...},
  deps: ['app']
});
```

6. Now, remove all the `<script>` tags from the `index.html` file and reference the `vendors/require.min.js` file. This file uses a `data-main` attribute to reference the config file (`main.js`).

```
<script type='text/javascript' src='vendors/require.min.js'
  data-main='main.js'></script>
```

Using RequireJS in our project

To convert our modules into RequireJS-compatible modules, we will define them using the AMD specification. This specification says that to define a module you need to call the `define` function. This function receives an array that contains strings. These strings represent paths or aliases from the configuration file for each dependency (files required in the module).

The second parameter that the `define` function needs is a function that will return the module. This function will have dependencies from the array as arguments. The good thing with this pattern is that code inside the `define` function will not be executed until all dependencies are loaded. The following is what the `define` function will look like:

```
define(['dependency1','dependendency2'],function(dependency1,depencen
cy2){
  //you can use depencencies here, not outside.
  var Module = //can be a literal object, a function.
  return Module;
});
```

The function should always return the module variable, or whatever the module needs to return. If we don't set the `return` statement the module will return an undefined value.

Defining the app.js file

When we defined the RequireJS configuration, we said that the entry point will be the `app.js` file. The following are the steps to create the `app.js` file:

1. Create the `app.js` file.

2. Set the array of dependencies. Map these dependencies as arguments in the function. There are some files that just execute code and they return an undefined value. You don't need to map these files if they are at the end of the list of dependencies.

   ```
   define([
     //LIBRARIES
     'bootstrap',
     'knockout',
     'koAmdHelpers',
     'ko.validation',
     'icheck',

     //VIEWMODEL
     'viewmodel',

     //MOCKS
     'mocks/product',
     'mocks/order',

     //COMPONENTS
     'custom/components',

     //BINDINGS
     'custom/koBindings',

     //EVENTS
     'events/cart'
   ], function(bs, ko, koValidation, koAmdHelpers,
     'iCheck', 'ViewModel) {
   });
   ```

3. Now define the body of the module. It will initialize global configurations and global behaviors. Finally, it will return the view-model:

   ```
   define([...],function(...){
   ```

```
//ko External Template Settings
ko.amdTemplateEngine.defaultPath = "../views";
ko.amdTemplateEngine.defaultSuffix = ".html";
ko.amdTemplateEngine.defaultRequireTextPluginName =
  "text";
ko.validation.init({
  registerExtenders: true,
  messagesOnModified: true,
  insertMessages: true,
  parseInputAttributes: true
});

$( document ).ajaxError(function(event,response) {
  console.error(response);
  alert("Error in the communication. Check the console!");
});

vm.activate();

return vm;
});
```

The first file has a lot of dependencies, which we should keep ordered. First we have defined the libraries, then the view-model, mocks, components, and finally events. Each of these files should also be defined as modules; when they are called, the dependencies will be loaded.

Notice how we have updated the template engine definition: the `defaultPath` value to define where the templates are, the `deffaultSuffix` value to define the extension of the templates, and the library used to load the templates (in our case text). Now, we should apply this pattern to the rest of the files.

Converting a normal module into an AMD module

To convert a normal module, we will perform the following steps. Always apply the same steps for all our modules. We need to wrap them into the `define` function, list dependencies, and return the module we returned in our old one.

1. Open the `viewmodel.js` file.

2. Create the `define` function:

   ```
   define([],function(){});
   ```

3. Add all dependencies:

```
define([
  'knockout',
  'models/Product',
  'models/Customer',
  'models/CartProduct',
  'services/ProductService',
  'services/CartProductService',
  'resources/ProductResource',
  'resources/OrderResource'
],function (ko, Product, Customer, ProductService,
  CartProductService, ProductResource, OrderResource) {
});
```

4. Export the module into the `define` function:

```
define([],function(){
  var debug = ko.observable(false);
  var showDebug = function () {
    debug(true);
  }
  ...
  var activate = function () {
    ProductResource.all()
      .done(allCallbackSuccess.bind(this));
  };
  return {
    debug: debug,
    showDebug:showDebug,
    hideDebug:hideDebug,
    ...
  };
});
```

When we write `knockout` as a dependency, RequireJS checks the configuration to find the alias. If the alias doesn't exist, it looks in the path we have set in the `baseUrl` attribute.

Now we should update all our files using this schema. Notice that elements that should be set as dependencies are the same elements we have set using the module pattern.

Applying RequireJS to components

We didn't modularize our bindings and components in the second part of the chapter. But this doesn't mean that we couldn't.

We can use RequireJS not just to create modules, but also to load files asynchronously. In our case, bindings and components don't need to return an object. When these files are loaded, they extend the `ko` object and their job is done. A similar case occurs with events. We initialize events and the work is done. So these files just need to be wrapped into the `define` function. Add dependencies and load them in the `app.js` file as we did in the previous section.

In the case of the `add-to-cart-button` component, the code in the file will be the following:

```
define([
  'knockout',
  'models/CartProduct',
  'services/CartProductService',
  'services/ProductService'
],function(ko, CartProduct,CartProductService,ProductService){
  ko.components.register('add-to-cart-button', {
    ...
  });
});
```

Applying RequireJS to mocks

In the case of mocks, we need to require the Mockjax and the Mockjson library, as follows:

```
define([
  'jquery',
  'mockjson',
  'mockjax'
], function ($, mockjson, mockjax) {
  $.mockJSON.data.PRODUCTNAME = [
    'T-SHIRT', 'SHIRT', 'TROUSERS', 'JEANS', 'SHORTS',
      'GLOVES', 'TIE'
  ];
  ...
});
```

Applying RequireJS to bindings

Bindings are easy to convert. They just have jQuery and Knockout dependencies, as shown in the following manner:

```
define(['knockout','jquery'],function(ko, $){
  //toggle binding
  ko.bindingHandlers.toggle = { ... };
  ...
});
```

Applying RequireJS to events

Finally, we need to update the events/cart.js file. The confirm order event needs to update the view-model. We can require the viewmodel as a dependency and access its public interface:

```
define([
  'jquery','viewmodel','services/CartProductService'
], function(vm, CartProductService) {
  "use strict";
  $(document).on("click","#confirmOrderBtn", function() {
    vm.showOrder();
  });

  $(document).on("click", ".add-unit", function() {
    var data = ko.dataFor(this);
    $(document).trigger("addUnit",[data]);
  });

  $(document).on("click", ".remove-unit", function() {
    var data = ko.dataFor(this);
    $(document).trigger("removeUnit",[data]);
  });

  $(document).on("addUnit",function(event, data){
    CartProductService.addUnit(data);
  });

  $(document).on("removeUnit",function(event, data){
    CartProductService.removeUnit(data);
  });
});
```

The limits of the application

Finally we have a modularized application. Nevertheless, it has some limitations:

* What is the behavior of the browser's back and forward buttons? If we try to use them our application doesn't work as it should.

* If we want to split our application into pages, do we always have to show and hide templates in the same page?

As you can see, there is a lot of work to do. Knockout is good, but maybe it needs to collaborate with other libraries to solve other issues.

There is a copy of the code developed in this chapter at `https://github.com/jorgeferrando/knockout-cart/tree/chapter6RequireJS`.

Summary

In this chapter, you learned how to build modules in our projects and how to load files on demand.

We talked about the module pattern and AMD specification to build modules. You also learned how to debug KnockoutJS applications with the Chrome extension, Knockout context debugger.

Finally, we saw that when the application becomes bigger, it will need many libraries to cover all the requirements. RequireJS is a library that helps us with dependency management. Knockout is a library that helps us to apply the MVVM pattern in our projects in an easy way, but big applications need other features that Knockout doesn't provide.

In the next two chapters, you are going to learn about a framework called Durandal. This framework that uses jQuery, Knockout, and RequireJS to apply the MVVM pattern. In addition, Durandal provides more patterns to solve other problems, like routing and navigation, and enables the addition of new features using plugins and widgets. We can say that Durandal is the big brother of KnockoutJS.

Durandal – The KnockoutJS Framework

Through six chapters, we have built a complete frontend application with the basic libraries.

We have used some libraries to achieve our objective:

- **Bootstrap 3**: To have a solid, responsive, and cross-browser base style in CSS3
- **jQuery**: To manipulate the DOM and communicate with the server side through AJAX
- **Mockjax**: To fake AJAX communication
- **MockJSON**: To create fake data
- **KnockoutJS**: To bind data and synchronize JavaScript data and views easily

We have also applied some design patterns to improve the quality of our code:

- **The reveal pattern**: To show the public interface of our objects and hide the private properties and methods
- **The module pattern**: To isolate our code and make it portable
- **The dependency injection pattern**: To improve cohesion and decrease coupling

Finally, we introduced a library that helps us to manage dependencies in our project, RequireJS.

In small projects you can work with just these libraries. When the project grows, however, handling dependencies becomes harder. The more libraries and styles you need, the more difficult it is to maintain all of them. Also, it becomes harder to maintain the view-model, which begins to have too many lines of code. Splitting the view-model results in writing more events to communicate them, and events make code harder to debug.

To solve all these problems, Rob Eisenberg (`http://eisenbergeffect.bluespire.com/`) and his team created **Durandal** (`http://durandaljs.com/`). Durandal is a framework that joins all the libraries and good practices you will learn henceforth.

In this chapter, you are going to acquire knowledge of the basics to start working with the Durandal framework. You are not going to work on your cart project in this chapter. This will continue in the next chapter. This chapter is about understanding how Durandal works and how it connects all the pieces to create web applications fast and easily.

It is important to mention that Durandal has been one of the simplest and fastest frameworks for building applications. When another good framework called AngularJS (`https://angularjs.org/`) announced its version 2.0, Eisenberg abandoned Durandal and became part of the AngularJS team. It was a big blow for the Durandal and KnockoutJS community. But recently, Eisenberg left the AngularJS 2.0 project and announced new versions of Durandal. So we can say that we are working with one of the best frameworks for developing modern, cross-browser, and fully-compatible web applications.

Installing Durandal

To install Durandal, follow these steps:

1. Go to `http://durandaljs.com/downloads.html`.
2. Download the latest version of the starter kit: `http://durandaljs.com/version/latest/HTML%20StarterKit.zip`.
3. Unzip it in your project folder.
4. Rename it as `durandal-cart`.
5. Add the Mongoose server to the project or use the server you feel comfortable with.

The starter kit will give you a very good starting point to understand how Durandal works. In the following projects we can start directly with the standalone Durandal library, but here we are going to analyze the parts of this framework carefully.

To dig further into Durandal, download the HTML Samples.zip file (http://durandaljs.com/version/latest/HTML%20Samples.zip), but it is up to you to test these interesting samples. The following are the contents of the starter kit:

- The starter kit contains three folders and an HTML index file.

- The app folder contains the application itself. This contains two folders: viewmodels and views.

- The viewmodels folder has all the view-models the application needs — usually one view-model per page.

- The views folder contains the HTML bound to each view-model — usually one view per view-model. However, you can compose views (you will see that this is the actual power of Durandal).

- The lib folder contains the Durandal framework and all the libraries that the framework depends on.

- Inside the durandal/js folder you will find a folder called plugins. You can extend Durandal using plugins. You can also extend KnockoutJS using components and bindingHandlers.

- There is another folder called transitions. Inside it you can add animations that can be fired when a transition between two pages is complete. By default, there is just one (entrance.js), but you can download more from the Internet or build your own ones.

- The index.html file will be the entry point to the JavaScript application.

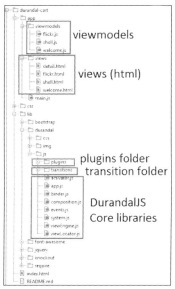

Durandal's folder structure

Durandal patterns

Before learning more about Durandal, let's learn about some patterns and concepts about the framework:

Durandal is a **Single Page Application (SPA)** framework. This means that:

- All web applications run on a single page (index page)
- There is no full-page refreshing; just the parts that change are updated
- Routing is not a server responsibility any more.
- AJAX is the basis of the communication with the server side

Durandal follows the Model-View-ViewModel (MVVM) pattern:

- Actually, it is called the MV* pattern because we can substitute the * with anything we use: View-model (MVVM), Controller (MVC), or Presenter (MVP). By convention, Durandal uses view-models.
- The MVVM pattern separates the view from the state (logic) of the application.
- The view comprises the HTML files.
- The view-models comprise JavaScript files bound to views.
- Durandal is focused on views and view-models. Models are not part of the framework. We should decide how they are built.

The framework uses the **Asynchronous Module Definition (AMD)** pattern to manage dependencies. It possesses the following characteristics:

- It uses RequireJS for this purpose.
- We should define one module per file.
- The name of the module will be the name of the file without the extension.

The index.html file

The `index.html` file is the entry point to the app. It should have a container with the ID, `applicationHost`. The application will run inside this container, and views will be interchanged:

```
<div id="applicationHost">
  <!-- application runs inside applicationHost container -->
</div>
```

You can define a `splash` element using the `splash` class. It shows when the application has completely loaded.

```
<div class="splash">
  <!-- this will be shown while application is starting -->
  <div class="message">
    Durandal Starter Kit
  </div>
  <i class="fa fa-spinner fa-spin"></i>
</div>
```

Finally, set the entry point of the Durandal application with RequireJS, as we set in the previous chapter. Set the `main.js` file as the entry point to the JavaScript:

```
<script src="lib/require/require.js"
  data-main="app/main"></script>
```

The main.js file

The `main.js` file contains the RequireJS configuration. Here we can see which libraries use Durandal to work:

- `text`: This is a RequireJS extension to load files that are not JavaScript files. Durandal uses `text` to load templates.
- `durandal`: This is the core of the framework.
- `plugins`: In this folder, we can find parts of the framework that are not required in all applications. These pieces of code can be loaded according to project needs.
- `transitions`: This contains the different animations we can play between page transitions. By default, we have just the entry animation.
- `knockout`: This is the library used to bind views and view-models.
- `bootstrap`: This is the design library related to the `bootstrap.css` library.
- `jQuery`: This is the DOM manipulation library.

You already have experience with RequireJS, since you converted files from your application to follow the AMD specification. This is how the `main.js` file containing the RequireJS configuration should look:

```
requirejs.config
({
  paths: {
    'text': '../lib/require/text',
    'durandal':'../lib/durandal/js',
    'plugins' : '../lib/durandal/js/plugins',
    'transitions' : '../lib/durandal/js/transitions',
    'knockout': '../lib/knockout/knockout-3.1.0',
```

```
    'bootstrap': '../lib/bootstrap/js/bootstrap',
    'jquery': '../lib/jquery/jquery-1.9.1'
  },
  shim: {
    'bootstrap': {
      deps: ['jquery'],
      exports: 'jQuery'
    }
  }
});
```

Then define the `main` module. Define dependencies in the same way you used RequireJS in your cart project:

```
define([
  'durandal/system',
  'durandal/app',
  'durandal/viewLocator'], function (system, app, viewLocator) {
    //main module code goes here
});
```

This module is where the application is configured. In the starter kit project, there is a default configuration that helps you understand what you can do at this point:

- Activate the debug (or not):

```
system.debug(true);
```

- Set the application title. The application title will be concatenated with the page title by default.

```
app.title = 'Durandal Starter Kit';
```

- Activate and configure plugins:

```
app.configurePlugins({
  router: true,
  dialog: true
});
```

- Start the application:

```
app.start().then(function() {
  //This code is executed when application is ready.

  //We can choose use framework conventions
  viewLocator.useConvention();
  app.setRoot('viewmodels/shell', 'entrance');
});
```

When you start the application, you can choose to follow Durandal's conventions. If you choose to follow them by default, Durandal will relate view-models with views by looking for views in the `views` folder. They should have the same name the view-model has. This means that if you have a view-model called `viewmodel/catalog.js`, its associated view will be called `views/catalog.js`.

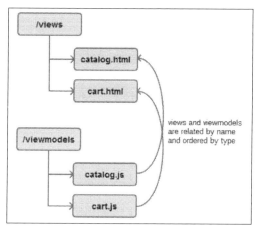

This is the file structure created by following Durandal conventions and is good for small and medium projects

This convention is good for small and medium projects. In big projects, it is recommended not to use Durandal conventions. If we choose not to use these conventions, Durandal will look for the view in the same folder that the view-model is in. For example, if the view-model is called `catalog/table.js`, the view should be named `catalog/table.html`. This allows us to group views and view-models by feature.

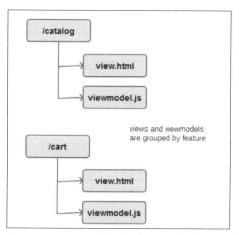

By not using Durandal conventions, we group our files by feature, which is good for big and scalable projects

Finally, indicate to the framework which view-model will start the application. By default, the shell view-model does this.

The shell view-model

Shell is the entry point module. It is the module that wraps the other modules. It is loaded just once and has the DOM elements that persist all the time.

To define a view-model, define a simple JavaScript object using the AMD pattern, as done in the following steps:

1. Define dependencies, that is, the router and the Durandal app:

   ```
   define(['plugins/router', 'durandal/app'], function
     (router, app) {
     return {
       //We complete this in next points
     };
   });
   ```

2. Expose the `router` method. The `router` method will give us an object that allows us to show the navigation bar easily.

   ```
   return {
     router: router
   };
   ```

3. Expose the `search` method. This is an optional method. It's part of the starter kit application. It manages the global search.

   ```
   return {
     router: router,
     search: function() {
       //easy way to show a message box in Durandal
       app.showMessage('Search not yet implemented...');
     },
   };
   ```

4. Expose the `activate` method. This is an important method in Durandal view-models. The `activate` method is fired when the view-model is ready. Here, you can request data to bind it to the view. We will see more about Durandal life-cycle methods soon.

   ```
   define(['plugins/router', 'durandal/app'],
     function (router, app) {
     return {
       router: router,
   ```

```
    search: function() { ... },
    activate: function () {
      router.map([{
        route: '',
        title:'Welcome',
        moduleId: 'viewmodels/welcome',
        nav: true
      }, {
        route: 'flickr',
        moduleId: 'viewmodels/flickr',
        nav: true
      }]).buildNavigationModel();
      return router.activate();
      }
    };
  });
```

The shell view

The **shell view** contains the navigation bar: the search bar and an element with an attached class called `page-host`. This element will be bound to the router, as in the following code. You can configure an animation to make the transition between pages cooler.

```
<div>
  <nav class="navbar navbar-default navbar-fixed-top"
    role="navigation">
    <!-- nav content we will explain then -->
  </nav>
  <div class="page-host" data-bind="router: {
    transition:'entrance' }"></div>
</div>
```

Durandal life cycle

It is important we understand clearly how a Durandal application works. This is a schema of how your application starts:

1. The `index.html` page uses RequireJS to request the `main.js` file.

2. The `main.js` file configures require and defines the main module, which is responsible for the application configuration, and launches the shell module.

3. The shell module handles the global context of the application. It manages components that will be persistent along the different life cycles. In the starter kit application, it manages the search bar. But it can also manage the log in and log out functionality, for example. The shell module is what configures all routes.

4. Finally, the router configures the navigation along all the pages the application has.

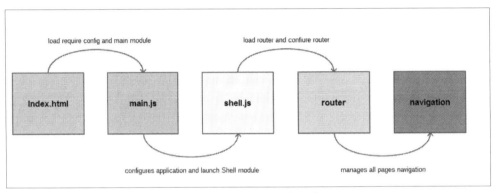

Durandal initialization life cycle

The activation life cycle

The **activation life cycle** controls the activation and the deactivation of the page. Durandal allows us to use predefined methods to access different parts of the cycle. Let's take a look at the Durandal methods:

- canDeactivate: This should return true, false, or as a redirect object. It is fired when you try to abandon a page. If the result of the method is true, you will be able to leave the page. If it is false, the routing process will be interrupted. If you return a redirect object, you will be redirected.

- canActivate: When you arrive at a new page, you can evaluate if you are able to see this page. For example, you can check if you are logged in to your if you have enough admin rights to see the page. If you return canActivate true, you will be able to see the page. If it returns false, the routing process will be interrupted. You can also redirect the user to another page.

- deactivate: If canDeactivate returns true and you can activate the next view, the deactivate method is fired. Here is a good place to clear timeouts and events, if necessary.

- activate: If canActivate returns true and you can deactivate the last view, the activate method is fired. Here is the place where you should load all your data, bind your elements, and initialize events.

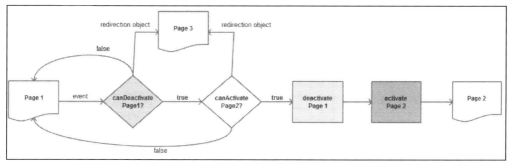

Activation life cycle

There are other methods we can use in our life cycle:

- `getView`: With this you can build an observable to define the path of the view that the view-model has bound.

- `viewUrl`: This returns a string that represents the path of the view attached to the view-model. The difference between `viewUrl` and `getView` is that the former is a string and the latter is an observable.

- `binding`: This is called before the binding between view and view-model begins.

- `bindingComplete`: This is called immediately after the binding is completed.

- `attached`: This is called when the composition engine attaches the view to the DOM. You can use this hook to manipulate elements using jQuery selectors.

- `compositionComplete`: This is the last hook fired by the composition engine. Here you can measure DOM elements.

- `detached`: This hook is fired when the view is detached from the DOM. We can perform clean up work here.

You can read more about the composition life cycle at `http://durandaljs.com/documentation/Interacting-with-the-DOM.html`.

The promise pattern

Durandal uses promises to manage asynchronous behaviors. A clear example is the `app.start()` method which is in the `main.js` file.

A promise is an object that contains a value that can be used in the future, when the prerequisites to obtain this value are accomplished. In this case, the `then` method will not be fired until the result `app.start()` method is obtained.

Internally, Durandal uses jQuery's promise implementation in order to minimize third-party dependencies. However, other libraries you use may require Q, or you may need more advanced asynchronous programming capabilities than jQuery can provide. In these cases, you will want to plug Q's promise mechanism into Durandal so that you can have a single consistent promise implementation throughout. To integrate the Q library, follow these steps:

1. Add the Q library to the RequireJS config.

2. Add this code in the `main.js` file, just before the `app.start()` instruction:

```
system.defer = function (action) {
  var deferred = Q.defer();
  action.call(deferred, deferred);
  var promise = deferred.promise;
  deferred.promise = function() {
    return promise;
  };
  return deferred;
};
```

If you are using the HTTP Durandal plugin, this approach will not be enough if you want to use Q promises. You need to wrap the jQuery promise into a Q promise, as follows:

```
http.get = function(url, query) {
    return Q.when($.ajax(url, { data: query }));
}
```

You can read more about the Q library at `http://durandaljs.com/documentation/Q.html`.

This is the basic interface of jQuery promises that we have available in Durandal:

- `done(successFn)`: This will be fired if the promise is resolved successfully.
- `fail(failFn)`: This will be fired if the promise is rejected.
- `always()`: This will be fired in both cases, success and failure.
- `then(succesFn, failFn)`: This is an alias to join `done` and `fail` methods.
- `when(valueOrFunction)`: This will create a promise with the value or function passed as a parameter.

To know more about jQuery promises refer to the official documentation at `http://api.jquery.com/promise/`.

Compositions

Composition is the most powerful part of Durandal. While modules help to split the application into small parts, compositions allows us to join them all again. There are two types of composition, object composition and visual composition.

To apply visual composition, you need to use the compose binding. You can combine KnockoutJS observables with the compose binding to achieve dynamic compositions. Compose binding gives you a complete configuration interface to enhance the flexibility and reusability of your components.

Object composition

You can achieve **object composition** by using just RequireJS and the AMD pattern. The simplest case is that you have two modules: A and B. The B module requires the functionality of A, so you request module A in module B using RequireJS, as follows:

```
//moduleA
define([],function(){
  var moduleA = {};

  //ModuleA code

  return moduleA;
});
//moduleB (in a different file)
define(['moduleA'],function(moduleA){
  //we can use ModuleA to extend moduleB, e.g:

  var moduleB = $.extend({}, moduleA);

  //Create moduleB unique functionality.
  return moduleB;
});
```

Visual composition

Visual composition allows you to break down your view into small pieces and reconnect (or compose) them, making them reusable. This is a central and unique function in Durandal and is managed by the Composition module. The most common manner of composing views is using the compose binding handler.

Let's take a look at how the shell view is composed:

1. RequireJS is used to find the shell module. By convention, it knows that it is in the `shell.js` file.

2. The view locator locates the appropriate view for shell: `shell.html`.

3. The view engine creates a view from the markup in `shell.html`.

4. The shell module and the shell view are data-bound together using KnockoutJS.

5. The bound shell view is inserted into the `applicationHost` div.

6. The "entrance" transition is used to animate the view.

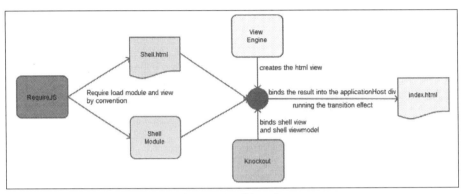

Composition life cycle

Now take a look how you can do some visual composition. You can move the navigation to its own view and compose the shell using the navigation view, by following these steps:

1. Open `shell.html` file.

2. Cut the `<nav></nav>` element.

3. Paste it in a new file called `navigation.html`.

4. Add a `<div>` in the `shell.html` file and bind the compose element, as follows:

```
<div>
  <div data-bind="compose: 'navigation.html'"></div>
  <div class="page-host" data-bind="router: {
transition:'entrance' }"></div>
</div>
```

You can also create a view-model called `navigation.js` linked to the view:

```
<div>
  <div data-bind="compose: 'viewmodel/navigation'"></div>
  <div class="page-host" data-bind="router:
    { transition:'entrance' }"></div>
</div>
```

You also have the option to convert the `compose` variable into an observable that will be generated in the view-model:

```
<div>
  <div data-bind="compose: navigationObservable"></div>
  <div class="page-host" data-bind="router:
    { transition:'entrance' }"></div>
</div>
```

This is a brief run-down about how the compose binding works:

- If it's a string value:
  - ○ If it has a view extension, locate the view and inject it into the DOM, binding against the current context.
  - ○ If it is a module ID, locate the module, locate its view, and bind and inject them into the DOM.
- If it's an object, locate its view and bind and inject them into the DOM.
- If it's a function, call the function with the new modifier, get its return value, find the view for the return value, and bind and inject them into the DOM.

If you want to customize the composition, you can pass the view and the model data directly to the composer binding, as follows:

```
data-bind="compose: { model:someModelProperty,
  view:someViewProperty }"
```

This allows you to combine different views with the same data, setting model or view as observables.

You can also compose views with Knockout comments:

```
<!-- ko compose: activeItem--><!--/ko-->
```

You can increase the setting values of the compose binding:

- `transition`: You can indicate a transition when the composition changes.
- `cacheviews`: This will not remove views from the DOM.
- `activate`: This defines the activate function for this composition.
- `perserveContext`: If you set this to `false` you will detach the parent context. This is useful when there is no model associated with the view. It improves performance.
- `activationData`: This refers to the data attached to the `activate` function.
- `mode`: This could be `inline` or `templated`. Inline is the mode by default. The `templated` mode is used with the `data-part` attribute and is often used with widgets.

- `onError`: You can bind an error handler function to fail gracefully when a composition fails as shown in the following code:

```
div data-bind="compose: { model: model,
  onError: errorHandlerFunction }"></div>
```

You can find a complete explanation of composition in the Durandal documentation at `http://durandaljs.com/documentation/Using-Composition.html`.

Router

Durandal provides a router plugin to make navigation quick and easy. The router works in cooperation with the history plugin to handle the navigation state in the browser.

To use the router plugin:

1. Activate the plugin in the `main.js` file:

```
app.configurePlugins({
  router: true,
});
```

2. Configure it in the `shell.js` file:

```
router.map([{...},{...}]).buildNavigationModel();
return router.activate();
```

Following is an example of how the router of our shopping cart application could be:

```
router.map([
  {route:['/*default route*/,'catalog'], title:'catalog',
    moduleId:'viewmodels/catalog', nav: true},
  {route:'cart', title:'cart', moduleId:'viewmodels/cart',
    nav: true},
  {route:'product/:id', title:'Product detail',
    moduleId:'viewmodels/product-detail', nav:false},
  {route:'product/:id*action', moduleId:'viewmodels/product',
    nav:false, hash:'#product/:id'},
]).buildNavigationModel();
return router.activate();
```

Take a look at the `shell.js` file. The router is passed as an element of the view-model. This allows you to update your navigation based on what the current route is. Durandal provides a friendly interface to build a navigation menu from a `router` object. Map routes in the shell activate hook and then, using the router fluent API, build the navigation model.

Finally, return the `router.activate()` method which contains a promise from the shell activate hook. Returning a promise means that the composition engine will wait until the router is ready before displaying the shell.

Let's look at route mapping in more detail. A route has different patterns. Minimally, you should provide a route and a `moduleId` value. When the URL hash changes, the router will detect that and use the route pattern to find the correct route. Then it will load the module with the `moduleId` value. The router will activate and compose the view.

There are some optional parameters:

- `nav`: When you call the `buildNavigationModel` method, it will create an observable array called `navigationModel` only with the routes that have this property set to `true`.
- `title`: This is used to set the document title.
- `hash`: With this, you can provide a custom hash to use for data-binding to an anchor tag. The router will generate a hash if none is provided.

There are four different types of routes:

- **Default route** is set as an empty string:

  ```
  route.map([{route:''}]);
  ```

- **Static routes** have no parameters:

  ```
  route.map([{route:'catalog'}]);
  ```

- **Parametrized routes** are routes with parameters:

  ◦ A parameter is defined with a colon:

  ```
  route.map([{route: 'product/:id'}]);
  ```

  ◦ Optional parameters are wrapped between parentheses:

  ```
  route.map([{route: 'product(/:id)'}]);
  ```

- **Splat routes** are used to build child routes. We can define them using an asterisk:

  ```
  route.map({route:'product/:id*actions'});
  ```

- **Unknown routes** are managed by the method:

  ```
  mapUnknownRoutes(module,view):
  ```

  ```
  route.mapUnknowRoutes(notfound,'not-found');
  ```

If you look in the `navigation.html` file you will be able to see how the router works.

Notice that the `foreach` binding against the `navigationModel` property router is built with the `buildNavigationModel` method. Each element of this array has an `isActive` flag, which is set to `true` when the route is active. Finally, there is a property called `isNavigating` that allows you to alert the user that navigation between pages is happening as follows:

```
<ul class="nav navbar-nav"
  data-bind="foreach: router.navigationModel">
  <li data-bind="css: { active: isActive }">
    <a data-bind="attr: { href: hash }, text: title"></a>
    </li>
</ul>
<ul class="nav navbar-nav navbar-right">
  <li class="loader" data-bind="css: {
    active: router.isNavigating }">
    <i class="fa fa-spinner fa-spin fa-2x"></i>
  </li>
</ul>
```

If you go back to the `shell.html` page, you will see that you attach a router binding to the `page-host` element. This binding displays the active route inside `page-host` container. This is just another demonstration of the power of Durandal composition.

Route parameters

Route parameters are set in the route using a colon. These parameters can be passed to the `canActivate` and `activate` methods of each module. If the route has a query string, it is passed as the last argument.

Triggering navigation

There are some ways to trigger navigation that have been enlisted here:

- Use an anchor tag:
  ```
  <a data-bind="attrs:{href:'#/product/1'}">product 1</a>
  ```

- Use the `router.navigate(hash)` method. This will trigger navigation to the associated module.
  ```
  router.navigate('#/product/1');
  ```

- If you want to add a new history entry but not invoke the module, just set the second parameter to `false`:
  ```
  router.navigate('#/product/1',false);
  ```

- If you just want to replace the history entry, pass a JSON object with the `replace` value `true` and `trigger` value `false`:

```
router.navigate('#/product/1',{ replace: true,
  trigger: false });
```

Child routers

In big applications, you must be able to handle maybe tens or hundreds of routes. Your application can just have one main router, but there is the possibility of it having multiple child routers. This provides Durandal a way to handle deep-linking scenarios and encapsulate routes by feature.

Typically, the parent will map a route with a splat (*). The child router will work relative to that route. Let's look at an example:

1. Require the application router.
2. Call the `createChildRouter()`. This will create a new router.
3. Use the `makeRelative` API. Configure the base `moduleId` and the `fromParent` property. This property makes the routes relative to the parent's routes.

This is how it works:

```
// product.js viewmodel
define(['plugins/router', 'knockout'], function(router, ko) {
  var childRouter = router.createChildRouter()
    .makeRelative({
      moduleId:'product',
      fromParent:true,
      dynamicHash: ':id'
    }).map([
      { route: 'create', moduleId: 'create',
        title: 'Create new product', type: 'intro', nav: true },
      { route: 'update', moduleId: 'update',
        title: 'Update product', type: 'intro', nav: true},
    ]).buildNavigationModel();
  return {
    //the property on the view model should be called router
    router: childRouter
  };
});
```

First, it catches the `product/:id*action` pattern. This will cause navigation to `product.js`. The application router will detect the presence of the child router and it delegate control to the child.

When a child router works with parameters, activate the `dynamicHash` property inside the `makeRelative` method.

Events

Events are used to communicate between modules. The event API is integrated into the `app` module and is very simple:

- **on**: To subscribe the view-model to an event

```
app.on('product:new').then(function(product){
    ...
});
```

- **off**: To unsubscribe the view-model from an event

```
var subscription =
    app.on('product:new').then(function(product){
    ...
});
subscription.off();
```

- **trigger**: To trigger an event

```
app.trigger('product:new', newProduct);
```

You can pass all event names to listen to all type of events:

```
app.on('all').then(function(payload){
    //It will listen all events
});
```

Read more about events at `http://durandaljs.com/documentation/Leveraging-Publish-Subscribe.html`.

Widgets

Widgets are another important part in the composition of Durandal. They are like view-models, with one exception. View-models can be singletons, and we usually prefer that they be singletons because they represent a unique page on the site. On the other hand, widgets are mainly coded with a constructor, so they can be instantiated as many times as we need. Therefore, when we build a widget we don't return an object as it occurs in view-models. Instead, we return a constructor and Durandal instantiates the widget.

Save widgets in `app/widgets/{widget_name}`. The widget should have a `viewmodel.js` file and a `view.html` file.

We are going to develop a widget called `accordion` to demonstrate how widgets work. This widget will be based in the jQuery collapse plugin that comes with Bootstrap.

Setting up widgets

Follow these steps to create a plugin:

1. Add the `bootstrap` library to the project. To achieve this, add it to the dependencies of the main module:

   ```
   define([
     'durandal/system',
     'durandal/app',
     'durandal/viewLocator',
     'bootstrap'
   ], function (system, app, viewLocator, bs) {
     //Code of main.js module
   });
   ```

2. Install the plugin. Register the widget plugin in the `main.js` file:

   ```
   app.configurePlugins({
     widget: true
   });
   ```

3. Create a directory called widget inside the `app` folder.
4. Add a subdirectory named `accordion`.
5. Add a file named `viewmodel.js` inside the `accordion` directory.
6. Add a file named `view.html` inside the `accordion` directory.

If you don't like Durandal's conventions, you can read more about widget configuration at `http://durandaljs.com/documentation/api#module/widget`.

Writing the widget view

To write the view, follow these steps:

1. Open the `app/widgets/expander/view.html` file.
2. Write this code following the bootstrap3 collapse template (`http://getbootstrap.com/javascript/#collapse`):

   ```
   <div class="panel-group" data-bind="foreach: {
   ```

```
        data: settings.items }">
      <div class="panel panel-default">
        <div class="panel-heading" data-bind="">
          <h4 class="panel-title">
            <a data-toggle="collapse" data-bind="attr:{
              'data-target':'#'+id}">
              <span data-part="header"
                data-bind="html: $parent.getHeaderText($data)">
              </span>
            </a>
          </h4>
        </div>
        <div data-bind="attr:{id:id}"
          class="panel-collapse collapse">
          <div class="panel-body">
            <div data-part="item"
              data-bind="compose: $data"></div>
          </div>
        </div>
      </div>
    </div>
  </div>
```

By writing the view first you can identify which variables you need to create in the view-model to complete the view. In this case, you will need an array of items that stores accordion elements. It will contain an ID for each collapsible element that will auto-generate inside the widget, the header text and the body.

Writing the widget view-model

To write the widget view-model, open the `viewmode.js` file in the `accordion` widget folder and write this code:

```
define(['durandal/composition','jquery'], function(composition, $) {
  var ctor = function() { };

  //generates a simple unique id
  var counter = 0;

  ctor.prototype.activate = function(settings) {
    this.settings = settings;
    this.settings.items.forEach(function(item){
      item.id=counter++;
    });
  };
  ctor.prototype.getHeaderText = function(item) {
```

```
      if (this.settings.headerProperty) {
        return item[this.settings.headerProperty];
      }

      return item.toString();
    };

    return ctor;
  });
```

As you can see, you return a constructor for the widget, not a view-model itself as you do with pages.

In this case, to manage the life cycle you just need to define the `activate` method to assign values and generate IDs. Remember that if you want to add some DOM modification with code, the attached method would be a good place to do so.

Registering the widget

To register the widget, you just need to register it in the main module (`main.js`):

```
app.configurePlugins({
  widget: {
    kinds: ['accordion']
  }
});
```

Building a page with Durandal

Now that you have learned all the basics of the Durandal framework, let's create a new page that will contain our widget and some basic data.

To define a new page in Durandal, always follow the same steps:

1. Define the route in the shell view-model:

    ```
    router.map([
    { route: '', title:'Welcome', moduleId:
      'viewmodels/welcome', nav: true },
    { route: 'flickr', moduleId: 'viewmodels/flickr',
      nav: true },
    { route: 'accordion', moduleId: 'viewmodels/accordion',
      nav: true }
    ]).buildNavigationModel();
    ```

2. Define the `views/accordion.html` file. Notice that inside the accordion binding you can define the `data-part` templates. Here, you are using the power of composition that Durandal gives you. By adding an `add` button, you are giving the widget the possibility of adding new elements.

```html
<div>
  <h2 data-bind="text:title"></h2>
  <div data-bind="accordion: {items:projects,
    headerProperty:'name'}">
    <div data-part="header">
      <span data-bind="text:name"></span>
    </div>
    <div data-part="item">
      <span data-bind="text:description"></span>
    </div>
  </div>
  <div class="btn btn-primary" data-bind="click:add">
    Add new project
  </div>
</div>
```

3. Define the `viewmodels/accordion.js` file. You have set `projects` as an observable array and initialized it in the `activate` method. The view-model is provided with an `add` function that triggers an event called `accordion:add`. This sends a message with the new tab values. The widget should listen to this event and create an action.

```javascript
define(['plugins/http', 'durandal/app', 'knockout'],
  function (http, app, ko) {
  return {
    title: 'Accordion',
    projects: ko.observableArray([]),
    activate: function () {
      this.projects.push(
      {name:'Project 1',description:"Description 1"});
      this.projects.push(
      {name:'Project 2',description:"Description 2"});
      this.projects.push(
      {name:'Project 3',description:"Description 3"});
    },
```

```
      add: function () {
        app.trigger('accordion:add',
        {name:'New Project',description:"New Description"});
      }
    };
  });
```

4. Define the event in the `widgets/accordion/viewmodel.js` file, updating the `activate` method:

```
ctor.prototype.activate = function(settings) {
  this.settings = settings;

  var _settings = this.settings;//save a reference to settings
  var items = this.settings.items();//get data from observable

  items.forEach(function(item){//manipulate data
    item.id=guid();
  });

  this.settings.items(items);//update observable with new data

  //listen to add event and save a reference to the listener
  this.addEvent =
    app.on('accordion:add').then(function(data){
    data.id = guid();
    _settings.items.push(data);
  });
};
```

5. Define the detached life cycle method to turn off `add` event once the widget is not on the screen:

```
ctor.prototype.detached = function () {
  //remove the suscription
  this.addEvent.off();
}
```

6. Launch the application and test the widget.

Summary

In this chapter, you were introduced to Durandal. Using a framework that has all the pieces perfectly connected, instead of a bunch of libraries, helps you to avoid rewriting the same code again and again. It means that thanks to Durandal, you can follow one of the basic principles of developers (Don't Repeat Yourself – DRY) easily.

You learned useful concepts, such as how to install and bring up a Durandal project. You also learned about how the life cycle of a Durandal application works.

One of the most powerful features of Durandal is the composition. You can compose interfaces very easy and it is almost transparent for the developer.

You learned how Durandal manages promises. By default, it uses jQuery promises but you saw that it is very easy to use other libraries like Q.

Finally, you developed a widget and integrated it into a view-model. While view-models are singletons, widgets are elements that you can instantiate several times. They are a powerful part of the Durandal composition.

In the next chapter, we will migrate step by step from our KnockoutJS cart into a Durandal Single Page Application.

8
Developing Web Applications with Durandal – The Cart Project

Now that we know how Durandal works, it is time to migrate our old application over to using our new framework. In this chapter, you will learn how to reuse the code we have used in the book in other projects and also adapt part of the code to the new environment.

Introduction

We are going to develop a completely new application in this chapter. However, we are going to reuse most parts of the code we developed in the last chapter.

One of the disadvantages of working just with Knockout was that our application needs to connect to many libraries as it grows. The application we have developed during this book is very small, but has enough complexity and we haven't handled an important problem like routing. Our application always lies on the same page. We can't navigate between order and catalog or between cart and catalog. We have our entire application on the same page, showing and hiding components.

Durandal connects some libraries you have learned in this book and makes it easy to connect to new ones.

Along the chapter, we are going to see some schemas with non-standard UML notation. Nowadays, agile methods do not recommend using UML deeply, but these kinds of diagrams help us to get a global and clearer view of the structure and requisites of our features. Also, to deploy views we will see some sketches and mockups of how the HMTL should be done:

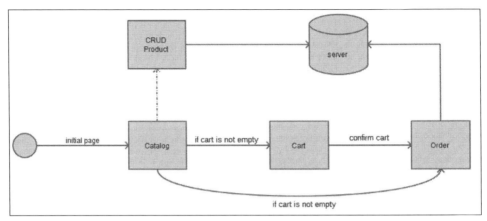

The life cycle of our application

Setting up the project

To start the new project, we are going to follow some steps that will give us a good starting point to develop our project:

1. Create a new project as we did with the Knockout cart.

2. Inside this project, copy the content of the Durandal Starter Kit project.

3. Now we should have three folders in our project:

    ○   app: This contains our application

    ○   css: This contains stylesheets

    ○   lib: This contains third-party libraries

4. Migrate the following libraries from the Knockout cart project to the Durandal cart project:

    ○   icheck

    ○   kovalidation

    ○   mockjax

    ○   mockjson

5. Install a new library called Toastr from http://codeseven.github.io/toastr/.

6. Update the ko.validation.js file on line 19 with the following code:

    ```
    define(["knockout", "exports"], factory);
    ```

7. Move the style.css file from the Knockout cart to the css folder in the Durandal cart project.

8. Move the `models` folder inside the `app` folder.

9. Move the `services` folder inside the `app` folder.

10. Create a file called `bindings.js` at the same level as the `main.js` file and move all the bindings inside the `koBindings.js` file there.

11. Create a file called `mocks.js` at the same level as the `main.js` file and move all mocks inside the `mocks` folder there.

12. Create a file called `components.js` at the same level as the `main.js` file and move all the components that are in the `components.js` file there.

13. Update the `knockout` library. The Durandal starter kit comes with version 3.1 and we are going to use 3.2, which is the version we used in the Knockout cart project. Version 3.2 allows us to use the `inputText` binding and components. You can see differences between all the versions at this link: `https://github.com/knockout/knockout/releases`.

14. Update the `main.js` file:

```
requirejs.config({
  paths: {
    'text': '../lib/require/text',
    'durandal':'../lib/durandal/js',
    'plugins' : '../lib/durandal/js/plugins',
    'transitions' : '../lib/durandal/js/transitions',
    'knockout': '../lib/knockout/knockout-3.1.0.debug',
    'bootstrap': '../lib/bootstrap/js/bootstrap.min',
    'jquery': '../lib/jquery/jquery-1.9.1',
    'toastr': '../lib/toastr/toastr.min',
    'ko.validation': '../lib/kovalidation/ko.validation',
    'mockjax': '../lib/mockjax/jquery.mockjax',
    'mockjson': '../lib/mockjson/jquery.mockjson',
    'icheck': '../lib/icheck/icheck'
  },
  shim: {
    'bootstrap': {
      deps: ['jquery'],
      exports: 'jQuery'
    },
    mockjax: {
      deps:['jquery']
    },
    mockjson: {
```

```
        deps:['jquery']
      },
      'ko.validation':{
        deps:['knockout']
      },
      'icheck': {
        deps: ['jquery']
      }
    }
  });

  define([
    'durandal/system',
    'durandal/app',
    'durandal/viewLocator',
    'mocks',
    'bindings',
    'components',
    'bootstrap',
    'ko.validation',
    'icheck',
  ], function (system, app, viewLocator,mocks,bindings,components)
  {
    //>>excludeStart("build", true);
    system.debug(true);
    //>>excludeEnd("build");

    app.title = 'Durandal Shop';

    app.configurePlugins({
      router:true,
      dialog: true
    });

    app.start().then(function() {
      //Replace 'viewmodels' in the moduleId with 'views' to locate
  the view.
      //Look for partial views in a 'views' folder in the root.
      viewLocator.useConvention();

      //Show the app by setting the root view model for our
  application with a transition.
```

```
        app.setRoot('viewmodels/shell', 'entrance');

        mocks();
        bindings.init();
        components.init();
    });
});
```

15. Set the project in your favorite server or copy the Mongoose executable in to the folder where `index.html` lies.

16. Update `index.html` with the new css file:

```
<link rel="stylesheet" href="lib/toastr/toastr.min.css" />
<link rel="stylesheet" href="lib/icheck/skins/all.css" />
<link rel="stylesheet" href="css/style.css" />
```

Now our project is ready and it is time to migrate our cart step by step.

Routing the project – the shell view-model

Durandal gives us the possibility of managing the routes in our project. We are going to split different parts of our project into pages. That will give a better user experience because we will be focused on just one task at a time.

We will split the app into four parts:

- The catalog
- The cart
- The order
- The product CRUD

These parts will contain more or less the same code we built in the Knockout application. Sometimes we will need to adapt small pieces of code.

To create these new routes, we will open the `shell.js` file and update the router:

```
router.map([
  { route: ['','/','catalog'], title:'Catalog',
    moduleId: 'viewmodels/catalog', nav: true },
  { route: 'new', title:'New product',
    moduleId: 'viewmodels/new', nav: true },
  { route: 'edit/:id', title:'Edit product',
    moduleId: 'viewmodels/edit', nav: false },
  { route: 'cart', title:'Cart',
```

```
        moduleId: 'viewmodels/cart', nav: false },
    { route: 'order', title:'Order',
        moduleId: 'viewmodels/order', nav: true }
]).buildNavigationModel();
```

Let's review how the router works:

- `route` contains the relative URL. In the case of the catalog, there are three URLs attached to this route. They are the empty route (''), the slash ('/') route, and the catalog. To represent these three routes, we will use an array.

- `title` will contain the title attached in the `<title>` tag.

- `moduleId` will contain the view-model that handles this route. If we use conventions, it will look for the view in the `views` folder, looking for the view which has the same name as the view-model. In this case, it looks for `views/catalog.html`. If we choose not to use conventions, Durandal will look in the same folder as the view-model.

- If `nav` is true, a link will be shown in the navigation menu. If it is false, the router doesn't display the link in the navigation menu.

The navigation and shell templates

As we did in *Chapter 7, Durandal – The KnockoutJS Framework*, we are going to compose our `shell.html` view in two parts: `shell.html` and `navigation.html`.

The catalog module

In the Knockout cart, we have a view-model that manages all parts of the application. Here we are going to split that big view-model into several parts. The first part is the catalog.

Here we have a schema of how it should work:

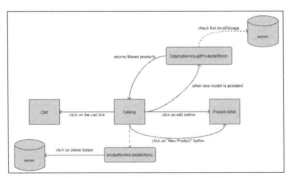

The workflow of the catalog module

Catalog will contain just the partial that includes the search bar and the table with its actions. This makes the view-model smaller and therefore more maintainable.

Although files will be split into different folders, catalog is a module by itself. It contains the view-model, the view, and some services that will only work inside this module. Other components will be required, but they will be shared by more modules along the live cycle of the application.

1. Create a file named `catalog.js` in the `viewmodels` folder and define a basic reveal pattern skeleton to begin adding features:

```
define([],function(){
  var vm = {};
  //to expose data just do: vm.myfeature = ...
  return vm;
});
```

2. Create a file named `catalog.html` in the `views` folder:

```
<div></div>
```

By just doing this, our module is ready to work. Let's complete the code.

The catalog view

We are going to use composition to create this template. Remember that composition is one of the powerful features of Durandal. To complete this feature, we will create three new templates that contain different parts of the root view. By doing this, we made our view more maintainable because we isolated different parts of the template in different files that are smaller and easy to read.

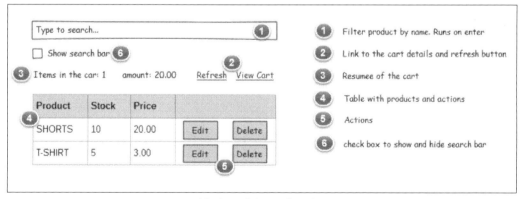

Mockup of the catalog view

Follow these steps to create the templates:

1. Open the `catalog.html` file and create the basic template:

```html
<div class="container-fluid">
  <div class="row">
    <div class="col-xs-12">
      <h1>Catalog</h1>
      <div data-bind="compose:
        'catalog-searchbar.html'"></div>
      <div data-bind="compose:
        'catalog-details.html'"></div>
      <div data-bind="compose:'catalog-table.html'"></div>
    </div>
  </div>
</div>
```

2. Create a view called `catalog-searchbar.html`. We prefix child views with the name of the root view, so if your editor orders files by name, they will be displayed all grouped together. We can also group all of them inside a folder. We can choose the way we feel more comfortable:

```html
<input type="checkbox" data-bind="icheck:showSearchBar"/>
  Show Search options<br/><br/>
<div class="input-group" data-bind="visible:showSearchBar">
  <span class="input-group-addon">
    <i class="glyphicon glyphicon-search"></i>
    Search
  </span>
  <input type="text" class="form-control"
    data-bind="value:searchTerm, valueUpdate: 'keyup',
    executeOnEnter:filterCatalog"
    placeholder="Press enter to search...">
</div>
<hr/>
```

3. Now it is time to define the view named `catalog-details.html`; it will contain actions and cart details:

```html
<div class="row cart-detail">
  <div class="col-lg-2 col-md-4 col-sm-4 col-xs-4">
    <strong>
      <i class="glyphicon glyphicon-shopping-cart"></i>
        Items in the cart:
    </strong>
    <span
      data-bind="text:CartService.cart().length"></span>
  </div>
```

```
<div class="col-lg-2 col-md-4 col-sm-4 col-xs-4">
  <strong>
    <i class="glyphicon glyphicon-usd"></i>
    Total Amount:
  </strong>
  <span data-bind="text:CartService.grandTotal"></span>
</div>
<div class="col-lg-8 col-md-4  col-sm-4 col-xs-4
  text-right">
  <button data-bind="click:refresh"
    class="btn btn-primary btn-lg">
    <i class="glyphicon glyphicon-refresh"></i> Refresh
  </button>
  <a href="#/cart" class="btn btn-primary btn-lg">
    <i class="glyphicon glyphicon-shopping-cart"></i>
    Go To Cart
  </a>
</div>
</div>
```

4. Finally, we will define the `catalog-table.html`, which contains the table we built in the Knockout cart project. Some `data-bind` elements should be updated and the footer needs to be removed:

```
<table class="table">
  <thead>
  <tr>
    <th>Name</th>
    <th>Price</th>
    <th>Stock</th>
    <th></th>
  </tr>
  </thead>
  <tbody data-bind="{foreach:filteredCatalog}">
  <tr data-bind="style:{color:stock() < 5?'red':'black'}">
    <td data-bind="text:name"></td>
    <td data-bind="{currency:price}"></td>
    <td data-bind="{text:stock}"></td>
    <td>
      <add-to-cart-button params="{cart:
        $parent.CartService.cart, item: $data}">
      </add-to-cart-button>
      <button class="btn btn-info"
        data-bind="{click:$parent.edit}">
        <i class="glyphicon glyphicon-pencil"></i>
```

```
        </button>
        <button class="btn btn-danger"
          data-bind="{click:$parent.remove}">
          <i class="glyphicon glyphicon-remove"></i>
        </button>
      </td>
    </tr>
    </tbody>
    <!-- FOOTER HAS BEEN REMOVED -->
  </table>
```

The catalog view-model

Now it's time to define all the components we can identify along our templates. We should begin defining the basic data we can locate inside the templates:

```
vm.showSearchBar = ko.observable(true);
vm.searchTerm = ko.observable("");
vm.catalog = ko.observableArray([]);
vm.filteredCatalog = ko.observableArray([]);
```

Once we define these variables, we realize that Knockout dependency is required. Add it to the dependencies array and also as a parameter in the `module` function:

```
define(['knockout'],function(ko){ ... })
```

Now we should define the `filterCatalog` method. It's the same method that we have in our view-model in the Knockout project:

```
vm.filterCatalog = function () {
  if (!vm.catalog()) {
    vm.filteredCatalog([]);
  }
  var filter = vm.searchTerm().toLowerCase();
  if (!filter) {
    vm.filteredCatalog(vm.catalog());
  }
  //filter data
  var filtered = ko.utils.arrayFilter(vm.catalog(),
    function (item) {
    var fields = ["name"]; //we can filter several properties
    var i = fields.length;
    while (i--) {
      var prop = fields[i];
      if (item.hasOwnProperty(prop) &&
        ko.isObservable(item[prop])) {
```

```
        var strProp = ko.utils.unwrapObservable(
          item[prop]).toLocaleLowerCase();
        if (item[prop]() && (strProp.indexOf(filter) !== -1)) {
          return true;
        }
      }
    }
  }
  return false;
});
vm.filteredCatalog(filtered);
};
```

The add-to-cart-button component was defined in the Knockout project and we don't need to touch any piece of code this component. This is a clear example of how good components are and the potential they have.

To edit a product from the catalog, we need to navigate to the edit route. This creates a dependency with the router plugin. We should add the plugins/router dependency to our module.

```
vm.edit = function(item) {
  router.navigate('#/edit/'+item.id());
}
```

To remove a product from the catalog, we will need to remove it from the server and also from the cart. To speak with the server, we will use the services/product. js file, and to speak with the cart, we will create a new service in a file named services/cart. Define the remove method:

```
vm.remove = function(item) {
  app
    .showMessage(
      'Are you sure you want to delete this item?',
      'Delete Item',
      ['Yes', 'No']
    ).then(function(answer){
      if(answer === "Yes") {
        ProductService.remove(item.id()).then(function(response){
          vm.refresh();
            CartService.remove(item);
        })
      }
    });
}
```

First we use the message component that Durandal has. It is very useful to handle modal dialogs. We will ask the user whether the product should be removed. If yes, we will remove it from the server and then refresh our view-model, and also remove the product from the cart because it is not available any more.

We should add a dependency to durandal/app and dependencies to ProductService and CartService.

ProductService was defined in the Knockout project. If we keep models and services very simple, they will become portable and adapt themselves very well to different projects.

Now is the time to implement the refresh method. We will call the ProductService.all() method and display a message letting the user know that the products are loaded. We will return the promise this method generates.

```
vm.refresh = function () {
  return ProductService.all().then(function(response){
    vm.catalog([]);
    response.data.forEach(function(item){
      vm.catalog.push(new
        Product(item.id,item.name,item.price,item.stock));
    });
    var catalog = vm.catalog();
    CartService.update(catalog);
    vm.catalog(catalog);
    vm.filteredCatalog(vm.catalog());
    LogService.success("Downloaded "+vm.catalog().length+"
      products", "Catalog loaded");
  });
};
```

Here, we use the same model for products that we used in the Knockout project. We are seeing a lot of code, but most of it was done earlier in the book, so we just need to move it from one project to the other.

The last step is to activate our view-model. When should a view-model be activated? When our products come from the server and are ready to be shown:

```
vm.activate = function() {
  if(vm.catalog().length === 0) {
    app.on("catalog:refresh").then(function(){
      vm.refresh();
    });
    return vm.refresh();
  } else {
```

```
        return true;
    }
}
```

The first time we load the application, we check to see whether the catalog has products. If it has, we just return that the catalog is ready. If the catalog is empty, we create an event that lets other services notify the catalog that it should be updated. Then we refresh the catalog to get new data.

This is the final result of our `catalog` view-model; of course we still need to implement the log service and the cart service:

```
define(['knockout','durandal/app','plugins/router',
    'services/log','services/product','services/cart',
    'models/product','models/cartproduct'
],function(ko, app, router, LogService, ProductService,
    CartService, Product, CartProduct){
    var vm = {};
    vm.showSearchBar=ko.observable(true);
    vm.searchTerm = ko.observable("");
    vm.catalog =ˉko.observableArray([]);
    vm.filteredCatalog = ko.observableArray([]);
    vm.CartService = CartService;

    vm.filterCatalog = function () {...};
    vm.edit = function(item) {...}
    vm.remove = function(item) {...}
    vm.refresh = function () {...}
    vm.activate = function() {...}
    return vm;
});
```

The cart service

The cart service will manage cart data for all modules. The services have persistent data along the session, so they can help us to share data between view-models. In this case, the cart service will share some pages with the cart: catalog, cart, and order.

The cart service will react to operations performed over the `cart` observable. The `add` operation is managed by the `add-to-cart-button` component but it would be interesting to integrate this behavior here. The refactoring of code can be a good exercise. In this example, we will keep the component and we will implement the other methods.

The cart service also stores the total amount of the cart in the grandTotal observable.

The cart service updates the cart as well. This will be useful because when the catalog is updated, product references stored in the cart are different from the new products in the catalog, so we need to renew these references. It also updates the catalog, decreasing the stock by the units of each product that are in the cart. We do this because the server sends us the data it has. The server doesn't know that we are shopping now. Maybe we decide not to shop, so the products we have in the cart are not registered as sold. This is why we need to update the units in the client once we get the products from the server. Here is the code of the cart service:

```
define(['knockout','durandal/app' ,'models/
cartproduct'],function(ko,app, CartProduct){
  var service = {};
  service.cart = ko.observableArray([]);
  service.add = function(data){
    if(!data.hasStock()) {
      LogService.error("This product has no stock available");
      return;
    }
    var item = null;
    var tmpCart = service.cart();
    var n = tmpCart.length;

    while(n--) {
      if (tmpCart[n].product.id() === data.id()) {
        item = tmpCart[n];
      }
    }

    if (item) {
      item.addUnit();
    } else {
      item = new CartProduct(data,1);
      tmpCart.push(item);
      item.product.decreaseStock(1);
    }

    service.cart(tmpCart);
  };
  service.subtract = function(data) {
    var item = service.find(data);
    item.removeUnit();
  }
```

```
service.grandTotal = ko.computed(function(){
  var tmpCart = service.cart();
  var total = 0;
  tmpCart.forEach(function(item){
    total+= (item.units() * item.product.price());
  });
  return total;
});
service.find = function (data) {
  var tmp;
  service.cart().forEach(function(item){
    if (item.product.id() === data.id()) {
      tmp = item;
    }
  });
  return tmp;
}
service.remove = function (data) {
  var tmp = service.find(data);
  var units = tmp.product.stock()+tmp.units();
  tmp.product.stock(units);
  service.cart.remove(tmp);
};
service.update = function (catalog){
  var cart = service.cart();
  var newCart = [];
  for(var i =0;i<catalog.length;i++){
    for(var j=0;j<cart.length;j++){
      var catalogItem = catalog[i];
      var cartItem = cart[j];
      if(cartItem.product.id() === catalogItem.id()){
        catalogItem.stock(catalogItem.stock() -
          cartItem.units());
        newCart.push(new
          CartProduct(catalogItem,cartItem.units()));
      }
    }
  }
  service.cart(newCart);
}
return service;
});
```

The log service

The log service allows us to display messages to inform the user about what is happening in our application. To do this, we use a library called Toastr. We can use Toastr directly on the application, but a good practice is to always encapsulate libraries to separate the code we should not touch. Also, wrapping the library in another one makes it easy to extend and customize the behavior of the library. In this case, we have also added the ability to log the message in the console:

```
define(["toastr"],function(toastr){
  //TOASTR CONFIG
  toastr.options.positionClass = 'toast-bottom-right';

  var error = function(text,title,log) {
    toastr.error(title,text);
    if (log) {
      console.error(title,text);
    }
  };
  var success = function(text,title,log) {
    toastr.success(title,text);
    if (log) {
      console.log(title,text);
    }
  };
  var warning = function(text,title,log) {
    toastr.warning(title,text);
    if (log) {
      console.warn(title,text);
    }
  };
  var info = function(text,title,log) {
    toastr.info(atitle,text);
    if (log) {
      console.info(title,text);
    }
  };
  return {
    error:error,
    success:success,
    warning:warning,
    info:info
  }
});
```

Adding products to the catalog

The add feature is related with this route:

```
{ route: 'new', title:'New product', moduleId:
  'viewmodels/new', nav: true }
```

To create this module, we need to create the add view and the add view-model. To do this, create two files called `views/new` and `viewmodels/new.js` and repeat the template we used with the catalog module.

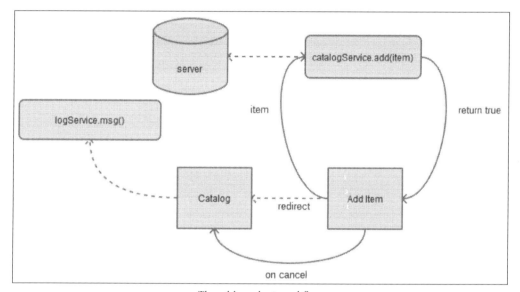

The add product workflow

The add product view

Creating or updating a product is more or less the same. The difference is that when we edit a product, the fields have data, and when we add a new product, the fields of this product are empty. This might make us wonder if maybe we can isolate views.

Let's define the `new.html` file as follows:

```
<div data-bind="compose:'edit.html'"></div>
```

This means the `new.html` file is composed by the `edit.html` file. We just need to define one template to manage both. Awesome, isn't it?

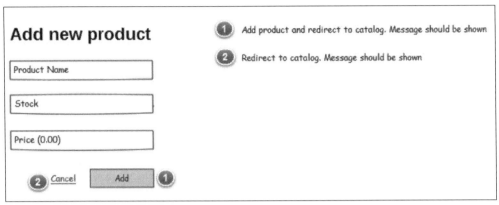

The add new product mockup

The edit view

We just need to copy and paste the edit form we had in the Knockout project. We have updated the layout, but we have used the same form:

```html
<div class="container-fluid">
  <div class="row">
    <div class="col-xs-6 col-xs-offset-3">
      <form class="form-horizontal" role="form"
        data-bind="with:product">
        <div class="modal-header">
          <h3 data-bind="text:$parent.title"></h3>
        </div>
        <div class="modal-body">
          <div class="form-group">
            <div class="col-sm-12">
              <input type="text" class="form-control"
                placeholder="Name" data-bind="textInput:name">
            </div>
          </div>
          <div class="form-group">
            <div class="col-sm-12">
              <input type="text" class="form-control"
                placeholder="Price" data-bind="textInput:price">
            </div>
          </div>
          <div class="form-group">
            <div class="col-sm-12">
              <input type="text" class="form-control"
                placeholder="Stock" data-bind="textInput:stock">
```

```
                </div>
              </div>
            </div>
            <div class="modal-footer">
              <div class="form-group">
                <div class="col-sm-12">
                  <a href="#/catalog"></a>
                  <button type="submit" class="btn btn-default"
                    data-bind="{click:$parent.edit,
                    enable:!errors().length}">
                    <i class="glyphicon glyphicon-plus-sign"></i>
                    <span data-bind="text:$parent.btn"></span>
                  </button>
                </div>
              </div>
            </div>
          </form>
        </div>
      </div>
    </div>
```

There are some things that should be created dynamically, such as the title of the layout and the button name. The `edit` method will say which method of the product service should handle the product— `ProductService.create` or `ProductService.save`.

The add product view-model

The add product view-model is coded in the `viewmodels/new.js` file. It will create a new product. If all is successful, we notify the user and navigate to the catalog. To show the new product in the catalog, we fire the `catalog:refresh` event:

```
define(["durandal/app","plugins/router","services/log","services/
uuid","services/product","models/product"
],function(app, router,LogService,uuid, ProductService,Product){
  var vm = {};
  vm.title = "New product";
  vm.btn = "Add product";
  vm.edit = function() {
    ProductService.create(vm.product.toObj()).then(function(response){
      LogService.success("Product added","New product "+vm.product.
name()+" added");
      router.navigate("#/catalog");
      app.trigger("catalog:refresh");
    });
  };
```

```
        vm.activate = function () {
          vm.product = new Product();
        };
        return vm;
      });
```

In the first version of our mocks, if we added a new project, our catalog wasn't getting updated. It returned the same five products we got at the beginning. We are going to improve our mock library to make it more realistic.

Making mocks real

Let's take a look at our mocks.js file, specifically the get products mock:

```
$.mockjax({
  url: "/products",
  type: "GET",
  dataType: "json",
  responseTime: 750,
  responseText: $.mockJSON.generateFromTemplate({
    "data|5-5": [{
      "id|1-100": 0,
      "name": "@PRODUCTNAME",
      "price|10-500": 0,
      "stock|1-9": 0
    }]
  })
});
```

Lets refactor this to:

```
$.mockjax({
  url: "/products",
  type: "GET",
  dataType: "json",
  responseTime: 750,
  responseText: updatedCatalog()
});
```

Now we are going to create the updatedCatalog function. We generate the array of products at the beginning and then we always work with this copy:

```
var catalog = $.mockJSON.generateFromTemplate({
  "data|5-5": [{
    "id|1-100": 0,
    "name": "@PRODUCTNAME",
```

```
    "price|10-500": 0,
    "stock|1-9": 0
  }]
});
var updatedCatalog = function () {
  return catalog;
}
```

In the old version of the mocks, when we got a product, we got one generated randomly using a template. Now we are going to come back with the real one. We will iterate along the catalog and return the product with the selected ID. Also, we will update the mock object. Instead of writing a response text, we will create a response function that will find the product and generate the correct response:

```
function findById(id){
  var product;
  catalog.data.forEach(function(item){
    if (item.id === id) {
      product = item;
    }
  });
  return product;
};
$.mockjax({
  url: /^\/products\/([\d]+)$/,
  type: "GET",
  dataType: "json",
  responseTime: 750,
  response: function(settings){
    var parts = settings.url.split("/");
    var id = parseInt(parts[2],10);
    var p = findById(id);
    this.responseText = {
      "data": p
    }
  }
});
```

We should update the POST and PUT mocks to add products to the mocked catalog and update the ones that exist:

```
var lastId= 101; //Max autogenarated id is 100
$.mockjax({
  url: "/products",
  type:"POST",
```

```
        dataType: "json",
        responseTime: 750,
        response: function(settings){
          settings.data.id = lastId;
          lastId++;
          catalog.data.push(settings.data);
          this.responseText = {
            "data": {
              result: "true",
                text: "Product created"
            }
          }
        }
      }
    });
    $.mockjax({
      url: "/products",
      type:"PUT",
      dataType: "json",
      responseTime: 750,
      response: function (settings) {
        var p = findById(settings.data.id);
        p.name = settings.data.name;
        p.price = settings.data.price;
        p.stock = settings.data.stock;
        this.responseText = {
          "data": {
            result: "true",
            text: "Product saved"
          }
        }
      }
    });
```

We should also remove products from our mock when the DELETE method is invoked:

```
    $.mockjax({
      url: /^\/products\/([\d]+)$/,
      type:"DELETE",
      dataType: "json",
      responseTime: 750,
      response: function(settings){
        var parts = settings.url.split("/");
        var id = parseInt(parts[2],10);
        var p = findById(id);
```

```
      var index = catalog.data.indexOf(p);
      if (index > -1) {
        catalog.data.splice(index, 1);
      }
      this.responseText = {
        "data": {
          result: "true",
          text: "Product deleted"
        }
      }
    }
  });
```

Finally, we should move the order mock to this file in order to share the catalog. When an order is performed, the stock in the catalog should be updated:

```
  $.mockjax({
    type: 'PUT',
    url: '/order',
    responseTime: 750,
    response: function (settings){
      var cart = settings.data.order();
      cart.forEach(function(item){
        var elem = findById(item.product.id());
        elem.stock -= item.units();
      });
      this.responseText = {
        "data": {
          orderId:uuid(),
          result: "true",
          text: "Order saved"
        }
      };
    }
  });
```

The order mock will generate a unique ID that identifies the order. This must be sent back to the user to identify the order in the future. In our application, this is the end of the life cycle of our project.

This is the uuid function we use to generate unique IDs:

```
  var uuid = (function uuid() {
    function s4() {
      return Math.floor((1 + Math.random()) * 0x10000)
      .toString(16)
```

```
          .substring(1);
    }
    return function() {
        return s4() + s4() + '-' + s4() + '-' + s4() + '-' +
            s4() + '-' + s4() + s4() + s4();
    };
})();
```

We can leave this function in the mock module or create a new service that handles unique ID generation.

Now our mock responds to the application in a more realistic way.

The edit view-model

Coming back to our modules, we now need to create the `edit.js` view-model. It will have the same structure as the `new.js` file, but in this case the activation will retrieve the product we are going to edit. Then we will save the product and the mock will update it on the (fake) server:

```
define(["durandal/app","plugins/router","services/log","services/
uuid","services/product","models/product"
],function(app, router,LogService,uuid,ProductService,Product){
    var vm = {};
    vm.title = "Edit Product";
    vm.btn = "Edit product";
    vm.activate = function(id) {
        return ProductService.get(id).then(function(response){
            var p = response.data;
            if (p) {
                vm.product = new Product(p.id, p.name, p.price, p.stock);
            } else {
                LogService.error("We didn't find product with id: "+id)
                router.navigate('#/catalog');
            }
        });
    };
    vm.edit = function() {
        ProductService.save(vm.product.toObj()).then(
            function(response){
            LogService.success("Product saved","Product
                "+vm.product.name()+" saved");
            router.navigate("#/catalog");
            app.trigger("catalog:refresh");
        });
```

```
    };
    return vm;
  });
```

We should notice that in both add product and edit product, the model is validated. We made this in the Knockout project and now we are reusing it in this project. Isn't it amazing?

The cart module

The cart module will manage the partial that shows the cart. As we did in the Knockout project, we should be able to update the quantity of the product. We will remove items if we don't want them anymore. Also, we will only activate this view if the cart has products in it, because it doesn't make sense to visit the cart if it is empty. In that case, we will be redirected to the catalog.

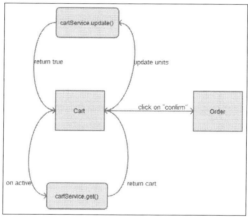

The cart workflow

The cart view

The cart uses the same template we used in the Knockout project. Of course we have adapted it a little bit to show it centered on the screen:

```
<div class="container-fluid">
  <div class="row">
    <div class="col-xs-8 col-xs-offset-2">
      <h1>Cart</h1>
      <div class="list-group" data-bind="foreach:cart">
        <div data-bind="compose: 'cart-item.html'"></div>
      </div>
      <button class="btn btn-primary btn-sm"
```

```
      data-bind="enable:cart().length,click:toOrder">
      Confirm Order
    </button>
  </div>
</div>
</div>
```

As we did with the cart item, we also compose the view here. The `cart-item.html`
file has the same code that is in the Knockout project. Just notice that `addUnit` and
`removeUnit` are now called by the parent:

```html
<div class="list-group-item" style="overflow: hidden">
  <button type="button" class="close pull-right"
    data-bind="click:$parent.removeProduct">
    <span>&times;</span>
  </button>
  <h4 class="" data-bind="text:product.name"></h4>
  <div class="input-group cart-unit">
    <input type="text" class="form-control"
      data-bind="textInput:units" readonly/>
    <span class="input-group-addon">
      <div class="btn-group-vertical">
        <button class="btn btn-default btn-xs add-unit"
          data-bind="click:$parent.addUnit">
          <i class="glyphicon glyphicon-chevron-up"></i>
        </button>
        <button class="btn btn-default btn-xs remove-unit"
          data-bind="click:$parent.removeUnit">
          <i class="glyphicon glyphicon-chevron-down"></i>
        </button>
      </div>
    </span>
  </div>
</div>
```

The cart view mockup

The cart view-model

The cart view-model will talk to the cart service and will update the state of the cart. Look how we are using the cart service to share information between modules. This is because we have created the service as an object and it is a singleton. Once it is loaded, it will persist during the application's life cycle:

```
define([
  'durandal/app','plugins/router','services/log',"services/cart"
],function(app, router, LogService, CartService){
  var vm={};
  vm.cart = CartService.cart;
  vm.addUnit = function(data){
    CartService.add(data.product);
  };
  vm.removeUnit = function(data) {
    if (data.units() === 1) {
      remove(data);
    } else {
      CartService.subtract(data);   -
    }

  };
  vm.removeProduct = function(data) {
    remove(data);
  };
  vm.toOrder = function() {
    router.navigate('#/order');
  }
  vm.canActivate = function () {
    var result = (vm.cart().length > 0);

    if(!result) {
      LogService.error("Select some products before",
        "Cart is empty");
      return {redirect:'#/catalog'};
    }

    return result;
  }
  function remove(data) {
    app
    .showMessage(
      'Are you sure you want to delete this item?',
      'Delete Item',
```

```
            ['Yes', 'No']
        ).then(function(answer){
          if(answer === "Yes") {
            CartService.remove(data.product);
            LogService.success("Product removed");
          } else {
            LogService.success("Deletion canceled");
          }
        });
      }
      return vm;
    });
```

There are two ways to communicate between components in Durandal, services and events. To share information between view-models, the best practice is to use services. If you want to send messages from one service to a view-model, or between view-models, you should use events. This is because services can be required inside a module and you can call them explicitly. Moreover, we can't access view-models from other view-models or services, which is why we need to send messages to them using events.

The order module

This module will manage the confirmation of our order. To complete an order, we need to introduce our personal data. We can only access the order page if we have something in our cart. Once we confirm our order, we will get a message from the server with the order ID. The product's stock will be updated and we will be able to continue shopping.

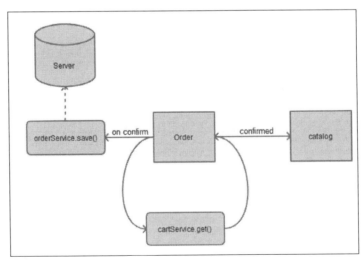

The order workflow

The order view

The order view will be the same order view we built in the Knockout project. This time we will use composition to make the view simpler.

The `order.html` file will contain the structure of the page and we will build some partials to compose the entire view. These partials will be:

- `order-cart-detail.html`: This will contain the read-only cart
- `order-contact-data.html`: This will contain the personal data
- `order-buttons.html`: This will contain the action buttons of the page

The `order.html` file will contain this code:

```
<h1>Confirm order</h1>
<div class="col-xs-12 col-sm-6">
  <div class="modal-header">
    <h3>Order</h3>
  </div>
  <div data-bind="compose:'order-cart-detail.html'"></div>
</div>
<div class="col-xs-12 col-sm-6">
  <div data-bind="compose:'order-contact-data.html'"></div>
  <div data-bind="compose:'order-buttons.html'"></div>
</div>
```

The `order-cart.html` file will contain the read-only cart. It's the same markup you can find in the `order.html` template in the Knockout cart project.

```
<table class="table">
  <thead>
  <tr>
    ...
  </tr>
  </thead>
  <tbody data-bind="foreach:cart">
    ...
  </tbody>
  <tfoot>
  <tr>
    <td colspan="3"></td>
    <td class="text-right">
      Total:<span data-bind="currency:grandTotal"></span>
    </td>
  </tr>
```

```
    </tfoot>
  </table>
```

The `order-contact.html` file will contain the form that is in the view `order.html`
Knockout cart project:

```html
<form class="form-horizontal" role="form" data-bind="with:customer">
  <div class="modal-header">
    <h3>Customer Information</h3>
  </div>
  <div class="modal-body">
    ...
  </div>
</form>
```

Finally, the `order-buttons.html` has the button to confirm the order. Of course, you
can find it in the `order.html` file we built in the Knockout cart project. We re-use as
much code as we are able to.

```html
<div class="col-xs-12">
  <button class="btn btn-sm btn-primary"
    data-bind="click:finishOrder,
    enable:!customer.errors().length">
    Buy & finish
  </button>
  <span class="text-danger"
    data-bind="visible:customer.errors().length">
    Complete your personal data to receive the order.
  </span>
</div>
```

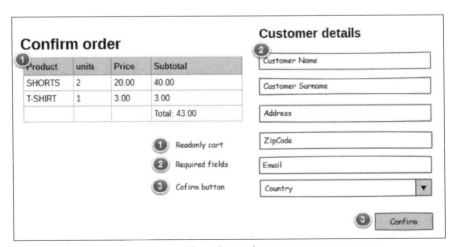

The order mockup

The order view-model

The order view will check whether our cart is empty to allow the activation. Validation is managed by the customer model. This model was built in the Knockout cart project. The rest of the code is partly from the big view-model we had in the Knockout cart project:

```
define(["knockout","durandal/app","plugins/router","services/log",
  "services/cart","models/customer","services/order" ],
  function(ko, app, router, LogService, CartService,
  Customer, OrderService){
  var vm = {};

  vm.countries = ko.observableArray(['United States','United
    Kingdom']);
  vm.cart = CartService.cart;
  vm.grandTotal = CartService.grandTotal;
  vm.customer = new Customer();
  vm.finishOrder = function () {
    OrderService.save({
      customer: vm.customer,
      order: vm.cart
    }).then(function(response){
      app.showMessage(
        "Your order id is:
          <strong>"+response.data.orderId+"</strong>",
        'Order processed successfully'
      ).then(function(){
        LogService.success("Order completed");
        CartService.cart([]);
        router.navigate("#/catalog");
        app.trigger("catalog:refresh");
      });
    });
  }

  vm.canActivate = function () {
    var result = (vm.cart().length > 0);

    if(!result) {
      LogService.error("Select some products before","Cart is
        empty");
    }

    return {redirect:'#/catalog'};
  }

  return vm;
});
```

Finally, our project is done and we have reused most of the old code. After migrating the project, we can see the advantages Durandal gives us. Notice also that we have not used the full potential of Durandal and Knockout. We can iterate over this project and improve all the parts again and again. We can create perfect isolated components. We can split the catalog into even smaller pieces and add more functionality, such as ordering and pagination. However, this project gives us a quick global overview of what Durandal is capable of.

Grouping code by feature – managing big projects

As you have seen in the `main.js` file, we are using Durandal conventions. This means that all our view-models lie in the `viewmodels` folder and all our views lie in the `views` folder. When we have a big project, having all the files in the same folder can be difficult to manage.

In this case, we remove the `viewLocator.useConvention();` statement from the `main.js` file. This acts as an indication to Durandal that all the views are in the same folder as the view-model.

We are going to group our project by features. We will define these features in our project:

- catalog
- cart
- order
- product
- shell

They will contain the code for each feature. Services, models, and other components will be as we had when we used conventions. Take a look at what the folders look like:

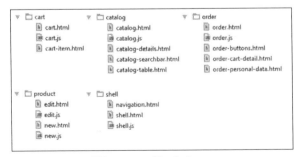

Files grouped by features

We need to update some code. The first step is to update the main folder, setting the new ID of the shell module:

```
app.setRoot('shell/shell', 'entrance');
```

Then we should do the same with the router inside the shell module:

```
router.map([
    { route: ['','/','catalog'], title:'Catalog',
      moduleId: 'catalog/catalog', nav: true },
    { route: 'new', title:'New product',
      moduleId: 'product/new', nav: true },
    { route: 'edit/:id', title:'Edit product',
      moduleId: 'product/edit', nav: false },
    { route: 'cart', title:'Cart',
      moduleId: 'cart/cart', nav: false },
    { route: 'order', title:'Order',
      moduleId: 'order/order', nav: true }
]).buildNavigationModel();
```

Finally, we need to update the compose paths. They should be full paths. This means that where we have the following code:

```
<div data-bind="compose:'catalog-details.html'"/></div>
```

We will now have the following code:

```
<div data-bind="compose:'catalog/catalog-details.html"/></div>
```

Our code will be ready to go.

Notice that now it is easy to find where the code we are working on is. Usually, we work on a feature and is more comfortable to have all the code of this feature in the same place. Also, we can better see whether we are isolating our feature properly. If we notice we are working too much out of the feature folder, maybe it means you are doing something wrong.

To see the code for this chapter, you can download it from GitHub:

- Durandal project using conventions from `https://github.com/jorgeferrando/durandal-cart/tree/chapter8part1`.

- Durandal project grouping files by feature from `https://github.com/jorgeferrando/durandal-cart/tree/master`.

Summary

Finally, we have developed a complete application that leads us to create Single Page Applications using Durandal.

During this book, you have learned best practices to work with the JavaScript code. These practices and patterns, such as the reveal pattern or the module pattern are used in all frameworks and libraries.

Building isolated and small pieces of code helps us to migrate our code easily from one environment to the other. In just one chapter, we have migrated our application from a basic Knockout application to a Durandal one.

Now we have developed good skills with Knockout and Durandal, we can try to improve this application by ourselves.

We can create a user module that enables users to log in and just allows administrators to edit and delete projects from the catalog. Alternatively, we can paginate our products and order them by price. We have acquired all the skills we need to successfully develop all these features. We just need to follow the steps you have learned during this book to complete these development tasks.

I hope that you have enjoyed this book as much I have. I would like to tell you that you need to push yourself to learn more about JavaScript, Knockout, Durandal and all the fantastic JavaScript frameworks that nowadays exist on the Internet. Learn the best practices and follow the best patterns to keep your code KISS and SOLID.

Index

Thank you for buying
KnockoutJS Essentials

About Packt Publishing

Packt, pronounced 'packed', published its first book, *Mastering phpMyAdmin for Effective MySQL Management*, in April 2004, and subsequently continued to specialize in publishing highly focused books on specific technologies and solutions.

Our books and publications share the experiences of your fellow IT professionals in adapting and customizing today's systems, applications, and frameworks. Our solution-based books give you the knowledge and power to customize the software and technologies you're using to get the job done. Packt books are more specific and less general than the IT books you have seen in the past. Our unique business model allows us to bring you more focused information, giving you more of what you need to know, and less of what you don't.

Packt is a modern yet unique publishing company that focuses on producing quality, cutting-edge books for communities of developers, administrators, and newbies alike. For more information, please visit our website at www.packtpub.com.

About Packt Open Source

In 2010, Packt launched two new brands, Packt Open Source and Packt Enterprise, in order to continue its focus on specialization. This book is part of the Packt Open Source brand, home to books published on software built around open source licenses, and offering information to anybody from advanced developers to budding web designers. The Open Source brand also runs Packt's Open Source Royalty Scheme, by which Packt gives a royalty to each open source project about whose software a book is sold.

Writing for Packt

We welcome all inquiries from people who are interested in authoring. Book proposals should be sent to author@packtpub.com. If your book idea is still at an early stage and you would like to discuss it first before writing a formal book proposal, then please contact us; one of our commissioning editors will get in touch with you.

We're not just looking for published authors; if you have strong technical skills but no writing experience, our experienced editors can help you develop a writing career, or simply get some additional reward for your expertise.

Mastering KnockoutJS

ISBN: 978-1-78398-100-7   Paperback: 270 pages

Use and extend Knockout to deliver feature-rich, modern web applications

1. Customize Knockout to add functionality and integrate with third-party libraries.

2. Create full web applications using binding preprocessors, Node preprocessors, and the Knockout Punches library.

3. In a step-by-step manner, explore the Knockout ecosystem by looking at popular plugins as well as the Durandal Framework.

KnockoutJS Starter

ISBN: 978-1-78216-114-1   Paperback: 50 pages

Learn how to knock out your next app in no time with KnockoutJS

1. Learn something new in an Instant! A short, fast, focused guide delivering immediate results.

2. Learn how to develop a deployable app as the author walks you through each step.

3. Understand how to customize and extend KnockoutJS to take your app to the next level.

4. Great examples showing how KnockoutJS can simplify your code and make it more robust.

Please check **www.PacktPub.com** for information on our titles

Building a Single Page Web Application with Knockout.js [Video]

ISBN: 978-1-78328-405-4   Duration: 01:51 hrs

Create a complete and structured single page application by doing more with less code using Knockout.js

1. Create a well-structured and organized application that you can build on and expand.

2. Learn how Knockout's data-binding can help you do more with less code.

3. Make use of best practices to ensure a maintainable code base.

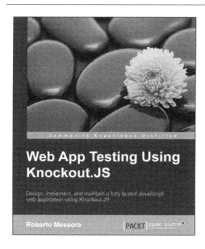

Web App Testing Using Knockout.JS

ISBN: 978-1-78398-284-4   Paperback: 154 pages

Design, implement, and maintain a fully tested JavaScript web application using Knockout.JS

1. Test JavaScript web applications using one of the most known unit testing libraries—Jasmine.js.

2. Leverage the two way bindings and dependency tracking mechanism to test web applications using Knockout.js.

3. The book covers different JavaScript application testing strategies supported by real-world examples.

Please check **www.PacktPub.com** for information on our titles

Printed in Germany
by Amazon Distribution
GmbH, Leipzig